OPERATIONAL RESEARCH

M. S. Makower, MA, Dip.OR, FSS, FOR, FInst.Pet., is Senior Lecturer in Operational Research and Head of the Department of Management Science at the University of Stirling. He has wide experience of OR applications, including projects in the oil, petrochemicals, rubber, electronics, mineral and steel industries, in Europe and North America.

E. Williamson, MA, Dip.OR, FSS, has worked as an operational research analyst in the steel and chemical industries, and as manager of the Port of London Authority's operational research unit. He is now Head of the Ports Section with the United Nations Conference on Trade and Development in Geneva.

TEACH YOURSELF BOOKS

OPERATIONAL RESEARCH

M. S. Makower and E. Williamson

TEACH YOURSELF BOOKS

Hodder and Stoughton

First edition 1967
Second edition 1970
Third edition 1975
Fourth edition 1985
Second impression 1987

P|c 1957

British Library Cataloguing in Publication Data

Makower, M. S.
Operational research.—4th ed.—(Teach
yourself books)
1. Operations research
I. Title   II. Williamson, E.
658.4′034   T57.6

ISBN 0 340 37100 5

Printed and bound in Great Britain for
Hodder and Stoughton Educational,
a division of Hodder and Stoughton Ltd,
Mill Road, Dunton Green, Sevenoaks, Kent,
by Richard Clay Ltd, Bungay, Suffolk.
Photoset by Rowland Phototypesetting Ltd,
Bury St Edmunds, Suffolk.

Contents

Preface

The object of this book is to increase the number of people familiar with some of the ideas of operational research. In order to do so without becoming too technical, we have adopted a problem-oriented approach without seeking to cover all of the philosophical, theoretical and managerial aspects of the subject. There are worked examples throughout the text. There are also further exercises (with solutions) at the end of each chapter. Thus those with a slight taste for numbers, and some recollection of school mathematics, should follow with ease the ideas presented.

There are no such things as operational research problems; there are just problems. The solution to some of these has involved the techniques we discuss. We hope that you will enjoy teaching yourself something about operational research.

M. S. Makower
E. Williamson

Acknowledgments

We are indebted to the Literary Executor of the late Sir Ronald A. Fisher, FRS, Cambridge; to Dr Frank Yates, FRS, Rothamsted; and to Messrs Oliver and Boyd/Longman for permission to reproduce, as our Table 2.6, Table III, the Normal Probability Integral, from their book *Statistical Tables for Biological, Agricultural, and Medical Research*. We are also indebted to the National Coal Board for permission to use an example from its book *Some Techniques of Operational Research* as our Example 5 in Chapter 8.

1

Operational Research

On 21 July 1969 man reached the moon. Twelve years later the space shuttle Columbia glided safely back to earth after orbiting the globe, thus heralding the era of the re-usable space craft, permanently manned space stations and commercial flights. These dramatic events have been made possible, after being mere fantasy not long ago, by the effective application of science. Knowledge of the motion of the earth and the moon, and of the nature of the surfaces of the two bodies, has been extended. Rockets and means of guiding them, and methods of sending and receiving signals from spaceships, have been developed. The astronauts have been given adequate protection and life-support systems. All this has reached an advanced degree of accuracy, control and reliability. By the scientific study of the whole environment in which an operation takes place, the important factors and their major interrelationships have been discovered, so that the desired objective may be achieved. This is operational research.

But are these space operations so very different from the running of a company, a transport service, an education authority or the police? The effective operation of such organisations also depends on having an understanding of the environment of the system, of the factors which affect the way the system operates and how they are related, and on having adequate channels of information and means of control. Thus the study of systems by scientific methods is developing rapidly in everyday, earth-bound contexts, as well as in space exploration.

The progress of a scientific study normally depends on experimenting with the system concerned. But how can we experiment with an organisation in the way that a physicist might with a pendulum? Clearly, experiments on organisations are likely to be very expensive, if not impossible. But this also arises, for instance, in experiments with the designs of ship hulls. Here the naval architect uses a model hull in a tank of water to test his ideas. As long as he is confident that his experimental results can be applied validly to a full-scale ship, he can then complete the final design and see the ship built. The operation of an organisation cannot be modelled in this direct way, but it can in a more abstract sense.

An example of an abstract model is provided by a two-part tariff that might be charged to domestic consumers of electricity. From the two rates charged the consumer can calculate how his electricity bill will depend on the number of units he consumes. A typical relationship is shown in Fig. 1.1.

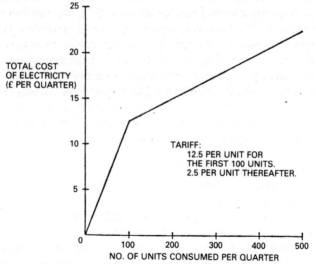

Fig. 1.1   Model of electricity costs, two-part tariff

This abstract model of electricity costs is used to predict exactly the total cost of any number of units that may be consumed during a quarter.

Many factors cannot be described as simply as these electricity costs. But some form of abstract model can be built up to describe the various operations of any organisation and how they are inter-dependent. Only with this information available is it possible to pursue the analysis and to determine what decisions will lead to improved performance of the organisation. The size and structure of many organisations means, however, that the people in them have neither access to all the necessary information nor the time to devote to such studies. Hence there is the need for the specialist activity of operational research, devoted to the study of operations.

As with other areas of endeavour, operational research must combine art, technology and science if it is to be successful. One is not concerned just with elegant, scientific descriptions of systems, as though they were specimens in a glass case to be admired. Rather one is concerned with studying a system in order to put forward policies which can be implemented in that particular situation and which will lead to a better performance of the system. One of the most difficult aspects may be in the establishment of the proper criterion of performance. Even having done this, one may have to be content with achieving an improved performance within a given time limit and budget, rather than taking longer to achieve a theoretically best performance. There are no such things as operational research problems; there are just problems. Some of these have been resolved by the approach illustrated in the chapters that follow.

2

Probability

Introduction

Operational research is concerned with problems which exist in the real worlds of business, government, the armed forces, etc. One of the features of this 'reality' is the existence of uncertainty. The breakdown of machines, the receipt of customers' orders at a factory, and the arrival of ships at a port are all, to some extent, unpredictable. A company cannot forecast its sales exactly; a government cannot predict exactly what revenue a proposed tax will yield; there is always an element of uncertainty. In dealing with such problems it is just as essential to obtain a measure of the uncertainty as it is to evaluate the expected outcome.

The branch of mathematics which deals with uncertainty is called statistics. We shall discuss in this chapter some of the more important statistical concepts necessary for a study of the techniques in the chapters which follow.

Frequency distributions

The first task in analysing quantitative information is to find some method of representing the data in such a way that the main features are readily apparent. The most useful way in which this may be done is by forming a frequency distribution. To illustrate how a frequency distribution is constructed and how, from it, important properties of the data are deduced, the information contained in Table 2.1 will be used. This table gives, for each of 100 students, two pieces of information: his weight and the number of motor accidents in which he has been involved.

These two quantitative characteristics are basically different in character. One of them, weight, is measured on a continuous scale and can take any value, within a certain range, on this scale. The only reason that the weights in Table 2.1 are given to the nearest kilogram is because this is the greatest accuracy to which it might be convenient to measure. Strictly speaking 69 kg includes all weights between 68·5 kg and 69·5 kg. A characteristic such as this which is measured on a continuous scale, is called a *continuous variable*. The number of accidents, however, must be a whole number – it is meaningless to speak of $2\frac{1}{2}$ accidents. A characteristic which can only take whole number values is called an *integer* or *discrete variable*.

By counting the number of observations which equal a certain value, a table may be constructed. If the variables are arranged in ascending order of magnitude, such a table is called a *frequency table*, and the distribution of values so formed is called a *frequency distribution*. In the case of the weights, however, these vary from a minimum of 59 kg to a maximum of 97 kg, i.e. a total range of 38 kg. When the range is so great, it is convenient to arrange the data in small groups, thus forming what is known as a *grouped frequency distribution*. Tables 2.2 and 2.3 overleaf are the frequency tables for the two variables, weight and number of accidents, respectively.

It is often useful to represent data in pictorial form. The most convenient method of doing this is to divide the horizontal axis of a graph into lengths corresponding to the values of the variable, and to construct a series of rectangles whose areas are proportional to the frequencies with which the values of the variable occur. Such a figure is called a *histogram* and Figs 2.1 and 2.2 show the histograms of the data contained in Tables 2.2 and 2.3 respectively.

The usefulness of histograms is that certain facts can be seen at a glance. From Fig. 2.1, for example, we see that the weights of the students are distributed fairly symmetrically around a value of about 78 kg, most of the weights being within a few kilograms of this value. The distribution in Fig. 2.2, however, is far from symmetrical, almost three-quarters of the students having had either one accident or none.

These observations, although useful, are still imprecise. It is

Table 2.1 Weights and number of motor accidents of 100 students

	Weight (kg)	No. of accidents		Weight (kg)	No. of accidents
1	78	1	42	67	1
2	78	0	43	78	2
3	66	1	44	73	3
4	78	0	45	79	0
5	71	0	46	84	0
6	80	1	47	79	2
7	75	0	48	79	1
8	88	1	49	77	0
9	77	1	50	64	2
10	66	1	51	90	1
11	72	2	52	75	0
12	59	3	53	80	0
13	73	0	54	71	1
14	83	1	55	77	2
15	74	3	56	97	3
16	80	2	57	69	1
17	89	1	58	81	0
18	75	0	59	76	0
19	71	0	60	62	0
20	70	0	61	74	2
21	76	2	62	69	1
22	77	1	63	87	2
23	82	0	64	81	1
24	82	0	65	77	0
25	79	1	66	75	0
26	74	1	67	76	3
27	75	1	68	94	2
28	83	2	69	74	1
29	70	0	70	78	2
30	79	2	71	75	0
31	72	3	72	81	1
32	78	1	73	72	0
33	84	0	74	78	0
34	81	4	75	76	1
35	80	1	76	73	0
36	92	1	77	84	0
37	68	2	78	91	1
38	80	2	79	85	0
39	78	4	80	87	1
40	76	1	81	65	3
41	74	0	82	71	1

Table 2.1 *contd.*

	Weight (kg)	No. of accidents		Weight (kg)	No. of accidents
83	68	5	92	85	0
84	78	0	93	77	0
85	74	1	94	79	0
86	82	0	95	86	1
87	72	1	96	79	0
88	82	2	97	73	1
89	75	0	98	82	0
90	77	1	99	76	0
91	77	0	100	79	0

Table 2.2 Frequency distribution of weights

Weight (kg) x		Frequency f
Range	Mid-point	
59–61	60	1
62–64	63	2
65–67	66	4
68–70	69	6
71–73	72	12
74–76	75	19
77–79	78	25
80–82	81	14
83–85	84	7
86–88	87	4
89–91	90	3
92–94	93	2
95–97	96	1
		100

Table 2.3   Frequency distribution of number of motor accidents

No. of accidents x	Frequency f
0	40
1	34
2	16
3	7
4	2
5	1
	100

possible, however, to express much of the information contained in a frequency distribution in just two quantities, or *parameters*, one which contains information on the size of the variables – a measure of location; and one which contains information on how scattered the variables are – a measure of dispersion. These two quantities are the *mean* and the *standard deviation*.

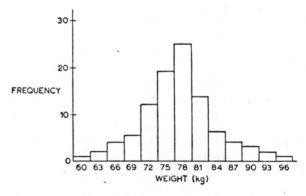

Fig. 2.1   Histogram of weights

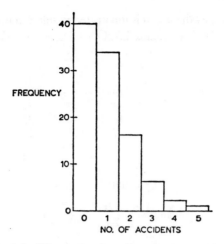

Fig. 2.2 Histogram of number of motor accidents

Mean

The mean of a frequency distribution is simply the arithmetic average value of the variables, i.e. the sum of the variables divided by the number of them.

If the value x_1 occurs with frequency f_1

    ,,   ,, x_2 ,,   ,,   ,, f_2

    ,,   ,, x_3 ,,   ,,   ,, f_3, etc.

then the sum of the variables is $f_1x_1 + f_2x_2 + f_3x_3$, etc. and the total number of variables is $f_1 + f_2 + f_3$, etc.

These expressions may be simplified by using the mathematical summation sign Σ (sigma). Thus

$$f_1x_1 + f_2x_2 + f_3x_3, \text{ etc.}$$

may be abbreviated to Σfx and $f_1 + f_2 + f_3$, etc., to Σf. Using this notation the mean is defined as follows:

$$\text{Mean } \bar{x} = \frac{\Sigma fx}{\Sigma f}$$

The calculation of the mean is illustrated in relation to the distributions given in Tables 2.2 and 2.3. Consider first the distribution in Table 2.3.

x	f	fx
0	40	0
1	34	34
2	16	32
3	7	21
4	2	8
5	1	5
	$\Sigma f = 100$	$\Sigma fx = 100$

$$\text{Mean } \bar{x} = \frac{\Sigma fx}{\Sigma f} = \frac{100}{100} = 1$$

The mean number of accidents per student is 1; a whole number in this case, but it need not be.

Before calculating the mean of the frequency distribution of weights, we can simplify the arithmetic by noting that if we subtract some constant value from every weight we shall be subtracting this same constant value from the mean. The calculation of the mean weight is made easier by subtracting 75 kg from all weights as follows:

x (kg)	$x - 75$	f	$f(x - 75)$
60	−15	1	−15
63	−12	2	−24
66	−9	4	−36
69	−6	6	−36
72	−3	12	−36
75	0	19	0
78	3	25	75
81	6	14	84
84	9	7	63
87	12	4	48
90	15	3	45
93	18	2	36
96	21	1	21
			372 −147

$$\Sigma f = 100 \quad \Sigma f(x - 75) = 225$$

$\Sigma f(x - 75)$ is the amount by which the sum of all weights exceeds an allowance of 75 kg per student.

$$\text{The mean excess weight} = \frac{\Sigma f(x - 75)}{\Sigma f} = \frac{225}{100}$$
$$= 2 \cdot 25 \text{ kg}$$

∴ the mean student weight is $75 + 2 \cdot 25$ or $77 \cdot 25$ kg.

Standard deviation

The standard deviation as a measure of variability about the mean is not such an obvious measure as the mean is of location, but it has important applications in statistical theory.

It is defined as follows:

$$\text{Standard deviation } s = \sqrt{\frac{\Sigma f(x - \bar{x})^2}{\Sigma f}}$$

The calculation of the standard deviation is illustrated in relation to the two distributions above. Consider first, again, the distribution in Table 2.3.

x	$x - \bar{x}$	f	$f(x - \bar{x})$	$f(x - \bar{x})^2$
0	−1	40	−40	40
1	0	34	0	0
2	1	16	16	16
3	2	7	14	28
4	3	2	6	18
5	4	1	4	16
		$\Sigma f = 100$		$\Sigma f(x - \bar{x})^2 = 118$

$$\text{Standard deviation } s = \sqrt{\frac{\Sigma f(x - \bar{x})^2}{\Sigma f}}$$

$$= \sqrt{\frac{118}{100}}$$

$$= 1 \cdot 09$$

The standard deviation of the number of accidents per student is $1 \cdot 09$.

This method of calculating the standard deviation is less straight-forward if the mean $\bar{x}$ is not a whole number, because then the quantities $(x - \bar{x})$ become fractional. There is an equivalent formula which is generally more convenient from the point of view of calculation. It can be shown that

$$\sqrt{\frac{\Sigma f(x - \bar{x})^2}{\Sigma f}} \quad = \quad \sqrt{\frac{\Sigma fx^2}{\Sigma f} - \bar{x}^2}$$

and it is this latter formula which is used in practice for the calculation of standard deviation. To illustrate the equivalence of the two formulae the calculation of the standard deviation of the number of accidents is repeated as follows:

x	f	fx	fx^2
0	40	0	0
1	34	34	34
2	16	32	64
3	7	21	63
4	2	8	32
5	1	5	25
	$\Sigma f = 100$		$\Sigma fx^2 = 218$

$$\text{Standard deviation } s = \sqrt{\frac{\Sigma fx^2}{\Sigma f} - \bar{x}^2}$$

$$= \sqrt{\frac{218}{100} - 1}$$

$$= 1 \cdot 09 \text{ as before.}$$

The standard deviation is a measure of the degree of scatter of the variables. Subtracting a constant value from every variable does not affect this scatter and therefore does not alter the standard deviation. The calculation of the standard deviation of weights may be simplified by using for x not the actual weights but the weights minus 75 kg.

The calculation is carried out on the opposite page.

We shall see later, in the section on the Normal distribution, just what significance the standard deviation has. Meanwhile, let us turn from an analysis of observed data, via an introduction to probability theory, to a study of some theoretical distributions.

x (kg)	f	fx	fx^2
−15	1	−15	225
−12	2	−24	288
−9	4	−36	324
−6	6	−36	216
−3	12	−36	108
0	19	0	0
3	25	75	225
6	14	84	504
9	7	63	567
12	4	48	576
15	3	45	675
18	2	36	648
21	1	21	441
	$\Sigma f = 100$		$\Sigma fx^2 = 4797$

$$\text{Standard deviation } s = \sqrt{\frac{\Sigma fx^2}{\Sigma f} - \bar{x}^2}$$

$$= \sqrt{\frac{4797}{100} - (2 \cdot 25)^2}$$

$$= 6 \cdot 55 \text{ kg}$$

Probability

We all have some understanding of probability. The purpose of this short introduction to the subject is to show how, instead of being able merely to express events as being improbable, more probable than not, or highly probable, we can express the degree of probability in quantitative terms. Probability may be defined as follows:

If there is evidence for believing that a particular outcome would occur on a fraction *p* of occasions in a large number of similar situations, then the particular outcome is said to occur with probability *p*.

If a particular outcome would *never* occur, $p = 0$, and this corresponds to one end of the probability scale – impossibility. If an outcome would *always* occur, $p = 1$, and this corresponds to the opposite end of the probability scale – certainty. For any outcome which may or may not occur, the probability must lie between these two extremes of 0 and 1.

An operation is performed to separate Siamese twins. The surgeon expresses his opinion that the operation has a 50:50 chance of success. What does this mean? It means that, in the surgeon's experience of similar operations, on only half of the occasions have both twins survived. The probability of the operation being successful is, therefore, $\frac{1}{2}$.

There are certain events whose very nature enables the probabilities of certain outcomes to be predicted. What is the probability, for example, that if a penny is tossed it will come down heads? From the symmetrical shape of the coin we suspect that the coin is equally likely to come down heads or tails and therefore the probability of heads is $\frac{1}{2}$. This concept of equally likely events leads to an alternative definition of probability, viz.:

If an event can occur in n mutually exclusive and equally likely ways, and if m of these ways lead to a particular outcome, then the probability of this outcome is

$$\frac{m}{n}.$$

For example, what is the probability that on being dealt a card from a well-shuffled pack it turns out to be a spade? 'A well-shuffled pack' implies that the card being dealt is equally likely to be any one of the 52 cards contained in the pack; thus $n = 52$. Only 13 of these cards are spades, therefore $m = 13$. The probability of a spade is, therefore, $\frac{13}{52}$ or $\frac{1}{4}$.

The laws of probability were originally developed to understand and predict the relative frequencies of various events in games of chance. There are two important laws of probability: the addition law and the multiplication law.

Addition law
The probability that an event will result in *any one* of several possible outcomes is the *sum* of the probabilities of the several individual outcomes, assuming all outcomes are mutually exclusive.

EXAMPLE 1

What is the probability of throwing a 4, 5 or 6 with one throw of a die?

Solution Any one of the above outcomes precludes both the others. Thus the outcomes are mutually exclusive.

$$
\begin{aligned}
\text{Probability of a 4, 5 or 6} = \ & \text{probability of a 4} \\
& + \text{probability of a 5} \\
& + \text{probability of a 6} \\
= \ & \tfrac{1}{6} + \tfrac{1}{6} + \tfrac{1}{6} \\
= \ & \tfrac{1}{2}
\end{aligned}
$$

Multiplication law

The probability that *all* of several events occur is the *product* of the probabilities of the several individual events, if the events are independent.

EXAMPLE 2

What is the probability of throwing three 6's in three throws of a die (or in one throw of three dice)?

Solution Throwing one 6 does not make it more or less likely that further 6's will be thrown. Thus the events are independent.

$$
\begin{aligned}
\text{Probability of three 6's} = \ & \text{probability of a 6} \\
& \times \text{probability of a 6} \\
& \times \text{probability of a 6} \\
= \ & \tfrac{1}{6} \times \tfrac{1}{6} \times \tfrac{1}{6} \\
= \ & \tfrac{1}{216}
\end{aligned}
$$

The following example illustrates the use of both the above laws of probability.

EXAMPLE 3

One bag contains three white balls and one black ball; another contains two white and three black balls. If one ball is taken from each bag, what is the probability that

(a) both are white?

(b) both are black?

(c) one is white and one black?

Solution

(*a*)   Probability that a white ball is taken from the
first bag $= \frac{3}{4}$

Probability that a white ball is taken from the
second bag $= \frac{2}{5}$

Probability that a white ball is taken from both
bags $= \frac{3}{4} \times \frac{2}{5}$
               $= \frac{6}{20}$ ✓

(*b*)   Probability that a black ball is taken from the
first bag $= \frac{1}{4}$

Probability that a black ball is taken from the
second bag $= \frac{3}{5}$

Probability that a black ball is taken from both
bags $= \frac{1}{4} \times \frac{3}{5}$
               $= \frac{3}{20}$ ✓

(*c*)   (i) Probability of taking a white ball from the first
bag and a black ball from the second
               $= \frac{3}{4} \times \frac{3}{5}$
               $= \frac{9}{20}$

(ii) Probability of taking a black ball from the first
bag and a white ball from the second
               $= \frac{1}{4} \times \frac{2}{5}$
               $= \frac{2}{20}$

The probability of one white and one black ball is
the sum of (i) and (ii). This is:

$$\frac{9}{20} + \frac{2}{20} = \frac{11}{20}$$

A check on these results is afforded by finding the probability that
one of the above outcomes occurs. This is:

$$\frac{6}{20} + \frac{3}{20} + \frac{11}{20} = 1$$

i.e. it is certain that one of these three outcomes occurs.

A few further exercises are given at the end of the chapter for the
reader to test his understanding of the laws of probability.

The binomial distribution

Consider an event which has just two possible outcomes: success or failure. The probability of a success is p and of a failure is q. (Since these are the only possible outcomes $q + p$ must equal unity.) What are the respective probabilities of 0, 1 and 2 successes if the event occurs twice?

Probability of no successes:
  This happens when a failure occurs on both occasions.
  The probability of this is

$$q \times q = q^2$$

Probability of 1 success:
  This can happen in two ways: either a success followed by a failure or a failure followed by a success.
  The probability of one success is, therefore,

$$pq + qp = 2pq$$

Probability of 2 successes:
  The probability of this is

$$p \times p = p^2$$

We notice that these probabilities are identical with the terms formed by the expansion of $(q + p)^2$, i.e. $q^2 + 2pq + p^2$.

Extending the analysis to the case where the event occurs three times, what are the probabilities of 0, 1, 2 and 3 successes?

Probability of no successes $= q^3$
Probability of 1 success $= pqq + qpq + qqp = 3pq^2$
Probability of 2 successes $= ppq + pqp + qpp = 3p^2q$
Probability of 3 successes $= p^3$

These probabilities are successive terms in the expansion of $(q + p)^3$, i.e. $q^3 + 3pq^2 + 3p^2q + p^3$.

It can be shown, quite generally, that if the event were repeated n times, the respective probabilities of $0, 1, 2, \ldots n$ successes would be given by successive terms in the expansion of $(q + p)^n$, i.e.

$$q^n, \quad npq^{n-1}, \quad \frac{n(n-1)}{2!}p^2q^{n-2}, \ldots p^n$$

(NB: 2! means 2 factorial, which is $2 \times 1 = 2$; 3! is $3 \times 2 \times 1 = 6$; $4! = 4 \times 3 \times 2 \times 1 = 24$; etc.) The expression $(q + p)$ is called a binomial and hence the distribution of probabilities formed by the expansion of $(q + p)^n$ is called the binomial probability distribution.

The numerical coefficients of the terms of $(q + p)^n$ are

$$1, n, \frac{n(n-1)}{2!}, \frac{n(n-1)(n-2)}{3!}, \text{etc.}$$

These coefficients may be obtained from an arrangement of numbers known as Pascal's Triangle, part of which is given in Table 2.4.

Each entry is this table is formed by adding together the two entries lying to the immediate north-west and north-east of it. For example, the entry 56 in line 8 is formed by adding together 21 and 35 in line 7.

Expressions for the probabilities of any number of successes may be written down by reference to Table 2.4. For example, the probabilities of $0, 1, 2, \ldots 7$ successes when an event occurs 7 times are, respectively, $q^7, 7pq^6, 21p^2q^5, 35p^3q^4, 35p^4q^3, 21p^5q^2, 7p^6q$ and p^7.

EXAMPLE 4

Four coins are tossed simultaneously. What are the probabilities of 0, 1, 2, 3, and 4 heads?

Solution   Since a coin is symmetrical in shape, $p = q = \frac{1}{2}$. The number of tosses n is 4.

$$\text{Probability of no heads} = \left(\tfrac{1}{2}\right)^4 = \tfrac{1}{16}$$
$$\text{,,} \quad \text{,,} \quad 1 \text{ head} = 4\left(\tfrac{1}{2}\right)^4 = \tfrac{1}{4}$$
$$\text{,,} \quad \text{,,} \quad 2 \text{ heads} = 6\left(\tfrac{1}{2}\right)^4 = \tfrac{3}{8}$$
$$\text{,,} \quad \text{,,} \quad 3 \quad \text{,,} = 4\left(\tfrac{1}{2}\right)^4 = \tfrac{1}{4}$$
$$\text{,,} \quad \text{,,} \quad 4 \quad \text{,,} = \left(\tfrac{1}{2}\right)^4 = \tfrac{1}{16}$$
$$\overline{1}$$

This distribution may be represented by a histogram as in Fig. 2.3.

Table 2.4 Pascal's Triangle of numbers

Coefficients in the expansion of $(p + q)^n$

n											
1	1	1									
2	1	2	1								
3	1	3	3	1							
4	1	4	6	4	1						
5	1	5	10	10	5	1					
6	1	6	15	20	15	6	1				
7	1	7	21	35	35	21	7	1			
8	1	8	28	56	70	56	28	8	1		
9	1	9	36	84	126	126	84	36	9	1	
10	1	10	45	120	210	252	210	120	45	10	1

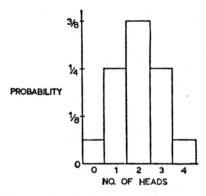

Fig. 2.3   Probability histogram of number of heads

Below is another one showing the frequencies of 0, 1, 2, 3 and 4 heads which we might expect if we tossed 4 pennies 160 times. If 'no heads' occurs with probability $\frac{1}{16}$, we should expect this event to occur on $\frac{1}{16}$ th of occasions in a large number of trials, i.e. 10 times in 160 tosses. Similar reasoning leads to the other frequencies of the histogram in Fig. 2.4.

We can now compare an idealised frequency distribution (which is what Fig. 2.4 is) with a theoretical probability distribution (Fig. 2.3). The two distributions are identical in shape and have an identical horizontal axis. Thus the means and standard deviations of

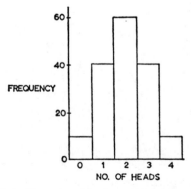

Fig. 2.4   Frequency histogram of number of heads

the two distributions are the same. The only difference between the two distributions is that the unit of the vertical axis of the frequency distribution is 160 (Σf) times that of the probability distribution.

We may calculate the mean and standard deviation of the frequency distribution as follows:

x	f	fx	fx^2
0	10	0	0
1	40	40	40
2	60	120	240
3	40	120	360
4	10	40	160
	$\Sigma f = 160$	$\Sigma fx = 320$	$\Sigma fx^2 = 800$

Mean
$$\bar{x} = \frac{\Sigma fx}{\Sigma f} = \frac{320}{160} = 2$$

Standard deviation
$$s = \sqrt{\frac{\Sigma fx^2}{\Sigma f} - \bar{x}^2}$$

$$= \sqrt{\frac{800}{160} - 2^2} = 1$$

Similar expressions to the ones above for the mean and standard deviation of the frequency distribution may be obtained for the mean and standard deviation of a probability distribution. Using μ (mu) for the mean and σ (sigma) for the standard deviation, and substituting p (probability) for f in the expressions above, we obtain:

Mean $\quad \mu = \dfrac{\Sigma px}{\Sigma p}$. Since Σp is 1, $\mu = \Sigma px$

Standard deviation
$$\sigma = \sqrt{\frac{\Sigma px^2}{\Sigma p} - (\Sigma px)^2}$$

$$= \sqrt{\Sigma px^2 - (\Sigma px)^2}$$

Since a theoretical probability distribution follows a fundamental law we need only carry through the calculation of the mean and standard deviation once, thereby obtaining an exact expression for these quantities. The mean value, Σpx, is given by the equation:

$$np \times \left(q^{n-1} + (n-1)pq^{n-2} + \frac{(n-1)(n-2)}{2!} p^2 q^{n-3} + \ldots + p^{n-1} \right)$$

as may be seen from the derivation below. The expression in the large brackets is the expansion of $(q + p)^{n-1}$. This is unity as $q + p = 1$.

No. of successes	Probability of x successes	
x	p	px
0	q^n	0
1	npq^{n-1}	npq^{n-1}
2	$\frac{n(n-1)}{2!} p^2 q^{n-2}$	$n(n-1)p^2 q^{n-2}$
3	$\frac{n(n-1)(n-2)}{3!} p^3 q^{n-3}$	$\frac{n(n-1)(n-2)}{2!} p^3 q^{n-3}$
.	.	.
.	.	.
.	.	.
n	p^n	np^n

Thus we are left with a simple expression for the mean of any binomial probability distribution, namely np. An extension of the above reasoning shows that the standard deviation of a binomial distribution is $\sqrt{npq}$. To confirm that the mean and standard deviation of the probability distribution in Table 2.3 is the same as that of the frequency distribution in Table 2.4 is a simple matter:

Mean $\quad\quad\quad\quad = np \quad\quad = 4 \times \frac{1}{2} \quad\quad = 2$

Standard deviation $\quad = \sqrt{npq} = \sqrt{4 \times \frac{1}{2} \times \frac{1}{2}} \quad = 1$

Expected value

In the context of statistics the expected value of a variable has a special meaning. It is a weighted average of all possible values of the variable, each value being weighted by its probability of occurrence. It is not necessarily the value we expect to occur; indeed in some cases the expected value is one which can never occur. For example, the expected value in throwing a die is $3\frac{1}{2}$. Although this value cannot occur it is the average of the numbers which turn up when the experiment is repeated many times.

EXAMPLE 5

A sample of five is taken from a large number of items known to contain 20% of items defective. What are the probabilities of 0, 1, 2, 3, 4 and 5 defectives appearing in the sample? What is the expected number of defectives in the sample?

Solution

Probability of a defective item, p, $= \frac{1}{5}$
Probability of a non-defective item, q, $= \frac{4}{5}$
Number of items in sample, n, $= 5$

The required distribution of the number of defectives in the sample is obtained by the expansion of $(\frac{4}{5} + \frac{1}{5})^5$ as follows:

Probability of no defectives $= (\frac{4}{5})^5$ $= 0\cdot328$
,,   ,,   1 defective $= 5(\frac{1}{5})(\frac{4}{5})^4$ $= 0\cdot410$
,,   ,,   2 defectives $= 10(\frac{1}{5})^2(\frac{4}{5})^3$ $= 0\cdot205$
,,   ,,   3   ,, $= 10(\frac{1}{5})^3(\frac{4}{5})^2$ $= 0\cdot051$
,,   ,,   4   ,, $= 5(\frac{1}{5})^4(\frac{4}{5})$ $= 0\cdot006$
,,   ,,   5   ,, $= (\frac{1}{5})^5$ $=$ negligible

$\overline{}$
                                          $1\cdot000$
$\overline{}$

The mean of the above probability distribution of defectives per sample is:

$$np = 5 \times \tfrac{1}{5} = 1$$

The expected number of defectives in the sample is, therefore, 1. Whilst the expected outcome is the same as the most probable outcome in this case, this is only coincidental. The expected outcome corresponds to the average value in the long run. The most probable outcome, however, corresponds to the most frequent value in the long run. These values will often be different. If the reader will turn back to page 10 he will see that the average number of motor accidents per student is one, whereas more students have had no accidents than have had one.

The Poisson distribution

Consider the following situation:

Between 10 a.m. and 12 noon a telephone switchboard handles a large number of calls. Throughout this two-hour period the average frequency of calls remains constant, i.e. in any small interval of time, Δt, there is some small probability p that a call will be received, and this probability is independent of where this time interval occurs. (The term 'small' implies that the probability of receiving 2 or more calls is negligible.)

We are now in a position to determine the probability distribution of the number of calls per minute as shown below.

Let n = the number of time intervals of length Δt in one minute.

Probability of:

no calls $= q^n$

1 call $= npq^{n-1}$

2 calls $= \dfrac{n(n-1)}{2!} p^2 q^{n-2}$

3 ,, $= \dfrac{n(n-1)(n-2)}{3!} p^3 q^{n-3}$

.   .
.   .
.   .

x calls $= \dfrac{n(n-1)(n-2)\ldots(n-x+1)}{x!} p^x q^{n-x}$

.   .
.   .

.   .

n calls $= p^n$

This is a binomial distribution with a small value of p and a large value of n. Such a distribution is known as the Poisson distribution.

The probability of x events $P = \dfrac{e^{-\lambda}\lambda^x}{x!}$

Strictly, the Poisson distribution is the special case of the binomial distribution where p approaches zero and n approaches infinity whilst np – the mean of the binomial distribution – equals a constant, λ (lambda). Thus λ is the mean of the Poisson distribution.

The Poisson distribution is a very important probability distribution in operational research because it has been found to describe a wide range of commonly occurring phenomena, including, in addition to the arrivals of calls at a telephone switchboard, the amount of radiation reaching a given portion of space in a given interval of time, the arrivals of customers at service points, the demands on a warehouse stock, the failures of certain components and the incidence of various forms of accidents. Many of these events lead to queuing situations. Queues are discussed fully in Chapter 6 where the importance of the Poisson distribution will be demonstrated.

The Poisson distribution, which, like the binomial distribution, is a discrete probability distribution, is related to a continuous probability distribution. In a situation like the telephone switchboard discussed above, one could describe the arrivals of calls in one of two ways. One way is the one described, i.e. to obtain a probability distribution of the number of calls arriving per minute. Another way is to obtain a distribution of the length of time between successive calls. Whilst the distribution of calls per minute is necessarily discrete (the number must be an integer) the distribution of the time interval between arrivals is continuous. It can be shown, although the proof is beyond the scope of this book, that if the number of calls per time period follows a Poisson distribution, then the inter-arrival time is distributed exponentially as in Fig. 2.5.

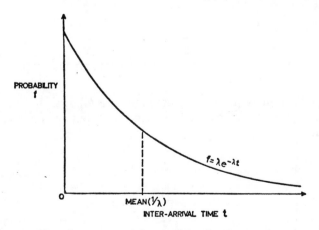

Fig. 2.5 Negative exponential probability distribution of inter-arrival time

The Poisson distribution describes only those events where the probability remains constant from one time period to the next. This implies that it is as likely that an event will occur just after several other events have occurred in quick succession as when a considerable time has elapsed since the last event occurred. Such a pattern of events is said to be 'purely random'. The reason for this description is that in all other event patterns there are always some intervals of time during which events are more probable than in others.

The original attempt to fit the Poisson distribution to 'random events' was for the number of cavalrymen killed by horse kicks during the course of a year. Table 2.5 shows in the second column the frequencies of the number of deaths per corps per year. Comparison with these data shows that the Poisson frequencies given in the third column are remarkably close.

Table 2.5   The numbers of men in ten Prussian Army corps killed by a horse kick in the twenty years 1875–94

Number of deaths	Observed frequency	Poisson distribution with same mean
0	109	109
1	65	66
2	22	20
3	3	4
4	1	1
	200	200

The Poisson frequencies are determined as follows.

The mean of the observed frequency distribution is first calculated:

x	f	fx
0	109	0
1	65	65
2	22	44
3	3	9
4	1	4
	$\Sigma f = 200$	$\Sigma fx = 122$

The mean number of deaths per corps per year

$$= \frac{\Sigma fx}{\Sigma f} = \frac{122}{200} = 0 \cdot 61$$

This actual mean is now equated to the mean of the Poisson distribution λ.

The probabilities of 0, 1, 2, 3, 4 and 5 events given by the Poisson distribution are next calculated.

Probability of 0 events		$e^{-\lambda} = e^{-0 \cdot 61}$	$= 0 \cdot 543$
,,	,, 1 event	$\lambda e^{-\lambda}$	$= 0 \cdot 331$
,,	,, 2 events	$\dfrac{\lambda^2}{2!} e^{-\lambda}$	$= 0 \cdot 101$
,,	,, 3 ,,	$\dfrac{\lambda^3}{3!} e^{-\lambda}$	$= 0 \cdot 021$
,,	,, 4 ,,	$\dfrac{\lambda^4}{4!} e^{-\lambda}$	$= 0 \cdot 003$
,,	,, 5 ,,	$\dfrac{\lambda^5}{5!} e^{-\lambda}$	$= 0 \cdot 001$
			$\overline{1 \cdot 000}$

Each probability is quite easily obtained from the previous one by multiplying by λ, $\lambda/2$, $\lambda/3$, $\lambda/4$ and $\lambda/5$.

If the probability of no deaths is $0 \cdot 543$, the expected number of times no deaths will occur in 200 occasions is $200 \times 0 \cdot 543$, i.e. 109 (to the nearest whole number). The remaining frequencies in the third column of Table 2.5 were deduced in a similar manner.

The Normal distribution

The two probability distributions examined so far, the binomial and Poisson distributions, have been discrete probability distributions. Many properties of natural phenomena, however, are measurable on a continuous rather than a discrete scale and hence we seek a probability distribution capable of describing such phenomena. The most important continuous distribution is the Normal distribution. A typical Normal distribution is shown in Fig. 2.6.

The curve is symmetrical and bell-shaped and the tails of the distribution extend (theoretically) infinitely in both directions.

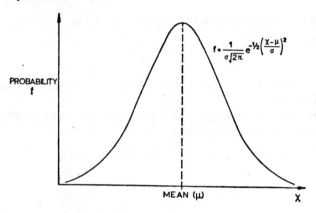

Fig. 2.6 The Normal distribution curve

There are many quantitative characteristics which are distributed in this way. One of the frequency distributions considered earlier – the weights of students – is approximately Normal in shape. Of particular importance is the fact that many types of error are distributed Normally. For example, 1-kg boxes of chocolates do not all weigh 1 kg. Closer examination would show that the actual weights are distributed Normally with a mean weight of a little over 1 kg. (If the mean weight is not a little over 1 kg the manufacturer risks prosecution!)

All Normal distributions are basically the same shape; they differ only by having different means and different standard deviations. By the following simple transformation we may cause all Normal distributions to coincide.

If we subtract the mean of a frequency distribution from every value of the variable, the result is a distribution having a mean of zero. If, in addition, we measure the variable not in its original units but using as the unit the standard deviation, the distribution will automatically have a standard deviation of 1. The result of applying this shift of origin and change of units to any distribution is to transform the distribution from one with a mean of μ and standard deviation of σ to one with a mean of zero and a standard deviation of 1. If the distribution is Normal the transformed distribution is called the *standardised Normal distribution*.

If the original variable is x and the new variable, formed as a result of this transformation, is z, the two are related by

$$z = \frac{x - \mu}{\sigma}$$

and z is simply the number of standard deviations that a value is away from the mean. A positive z indicates a value greater than the mean whilst a negative z indicates a value less than the mean. Fig. 2.7 shows the standardised Normal curve.

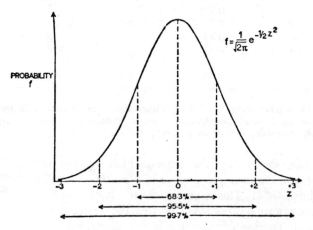

Fig. 2.7   The standardised Normal distribution

The scale of the vertical axis is chosen in order to make the total area lying underneath the curve equal to 1, and therefore the area lying under the curve and between any two values of z represents the probability that a value lies between these two values of z. It can be shown that

68·3% of the distribution lies between $z = -1$ and $z = +1$
95·5%   ,,   ,,   ,, $z = -2$ and $z = +2$
and   ,,
99·7%   ,,   ,,   ,, $z = -3$ and $z = +3$

Table 2.6 gives an abbreviated tabulation of the standardised Normal distribution.

Table 2.6 The standardisation Normal distribution

z	Probability of a value < z	z	Probability of a value < z
0·0	0·500	1·3	0·903
0·1	0·540	1·4	0·919
0·2	0·579	1·5	0·933
0·3	0·618	1·6	0·945
0·4	0·655	1·7	0·955
0·5	0·691	1·8	0·964
0·6	0·726	1·9	0·971
0·7	0·758	2·0	0·977
0·8	0·788	2·1	0·982
0·9	0·816	2·2	0·986
1·0	0·841	2·3	0·989
1·1	0·864	2·4	0·992
1·2	0·885	2·5	0·994

(Table 2.6 is taken from Table III of Fisher and Yates's *Statistical Tables for Biological, Agricultural, and Medical Research*, published by Oliver & Boyd/ Longman, by permission of the authors and publishers.)

The table shows the probabilities of obtaining values of z less than those given. For example, a value of z less than +1 will occur with probability 0·841. This is equivalent to saying that 84·1% of the values of a normal variable are less than the mean plus one standard deviation. The use of this table is best illustrated by one or two examples.

EXAMPLE 6
A survey indicated that men's weights are distributed Normally with a mean of 78 kg and a standard deviation of 7·5 kg. This being so, what proportion of weights are

(a) over 90 kg?
(b) between 63 kg and 78 kg?

Solution
(a) 90 kg must first be converted to standardised units.

$$z = \frac{90 - 78}{7.5} = 1.6$$

(i.e. 90 kg is 1·6 standard deviations above the mean). The probability that a value of z is less than 1·6 may be read from Table 2.6. It is 0·945. The probability that a value is greater than 1·6 is obtained by subtracting 0·945 from 1, i.e. 0·055. Thus 5·5% of men are heavier than 90 kg.

(b) 78 kg is the mean of the distribution and hence the corresponding value of z is 0. 63 kg is converted to standardised units as follows:

$$z = \frac{63 - 78}{7·5} = -2$$

(i.e. 63 kg is 2 standard deviations below the mean).

Because the distribution is symmetrical, as many values of z are between 0 and +2 as between 0 and −2. We therefore require the probability that a value of z lies between 0 and +2. From Table 2.6 the probability that a value is less than 2 is 0·977 and the probability that a value is less than 0 is 0·500.

Therefore, the probability that a value lies between 0 and 2 is 0·977 − 0·500 or 0·477. Thus 47·7% of men have weights between 63 kg and 78 kg.

EXAMPLE 7

The time when a country bus passes a certain point is distributed Normally with a mean of 9.25 a.m. and a standard deviation of 3 minutes. What is the latest time one could arrive at this point and still have a probability of 0·99 of catching the bus?

Solution The value of z which is exceeded on all but 1% of occasions is minus the value of z which is only exceeded with probability 0·01. From Table 2.6 this value of z is seen to lie between 2·3 and 2·4 and is approximately $2\frac{1}{3}$.

If $z = \frac{x - \mu}{\sigma}$, $x = \mu + z\sigma$.

In the above example

$$x = 9.25 \text{ a.m.} - \tfrac{7}{3} \times 3 \text{ min} = 9.18 \text{ a.m.}$$

Thus this is the latest time one could arrive and still have the desired probability of catching the bus.

It can be shown that the binomial distribution becomes closer and closer to the Normal distribution as n gets larger. The Normal distribution is usually an adequate approximation to the binomial if both np and nq are greater than 5.

The following example shows how useful this approximation is.

EXAMPLE 8

A coin is tossed 10 times. Find the probability of 3, 4 or 5 heads using

(*a*) the binomial distribution
(*b*) the Normal approximation.

Solution $n = 10$ and, since the coin is symmetrical, $p = q = \frac{1}{2}$.

(*a*) Probability of 3 heads $= 120(\frac{1}{2})^3(\frac{1}{2})^7 = 0\cdot117$

,,   ,, 4   ,, $= 210(\frac{1}{2})^4(\frac{1}{2})^6 = 0\cdot205$

,,   ,, 5   ,, $= 252(\frac{1}{2})^5(\frac{1}{2})^5 = 0\cdot246$

$\therefore$ Probability of 3, 4 or 5 heads $= 0\cdot568$

(*b*) Before using the Normal distribution we must note that because we are using a continuous distribution to approximate to a discrete distribution, we should evaluate the probability of a value lying between $2\frac{1}{2}$ and $5\frac{1}{2}$.

$2\frac{1}{2}$ is converted to standardised units as follows:

$$z = \frac{2\frac{1}{2} - np}{\sqrt{npq}} = \frac{2\frac{1}{2} - 5}{\sqrt{2\frac{1}{2}}} = -1\cdot58$$

Similarly, the standardised value for $5\frac{1}{2}$ is

$$\frac{5\frac{1}{2} - 5}{\sqrt{2\frac{1}{2}}} = 0\cdot32$$

To find the area of the Normal curve between $-1\cdot58$ and $+0\cdot32$ we must find separately the area between $1\cdot58$ and 0, and between $0\cdot32$ and 0.

Estimating these readings from Table 2.6, the

area between $1\cdot58$ and 0 is $0\cdot943 - 0\cdot500 = 0\cdot443$

,,   ,, $0\cdot32$,, 0 ,, $0\cdot625 - 0\cdot500 = 0\cdot125$

thus the area between $-1\cdot58$ and $0\cdot32$ is $0\cdot568$

This accords with the probability of 3, 4 or 5 heads given by the binomial distribution.

The usefulness of this approximation to the binomial distribution becomes increasingly apparent as n becomes larger. This is because, in addition to the approximation being closer the larger n is, the probabilities given by the binomial distribution become increasingly tedious to compute.

Exercises

2.1 Two cards are drawn at random from a well-shuffled pack. What is the probability of obtaining:

    (*a*) two cards of the same colour?
    (*b*) two of the same suit?

2.2 What is the probability that in five tosses of a coin no two successive tosses yield the same result?

2.3 Four torpedoes are fired at a ship, each having a probability of $\frac{1}{4}$ of hitting the ship. What is the probability that the ship is hit?

2.4 Suppose that in flight an aircraft engine has a probability of failure of 0·01 and that an aircraft can make a satisfactory landing if at least half of its engines function. What is the probability of:

    (*a*) a two-engined aircraft
    (*b*) a four-engined aircraft

crashing due to engine failure?

2.5 What proportion of families having six children would you expect to have three boys and three girls?

2.6 The following table shows the demand for a particular make of battery in a 100-day period.

Number requested	Frequency
0	25
1	30
2	24
3	14
4	5
5	2
	100

Calculate the mean and standard deviation of this distribution and calculate the frequencies given by the Poisson distribution with the same mean.

2.7 The mean inside diameter of a large sample of washers produced by a machine is 0·502 cm and the standard deviation is 0·005 cm. The purpose for which the washers are made allows a maximum tolerance in the diameter of 0·492 cm to 0·508 cm.

Determine the percentage of defective washers produced, assuming the diameters are distributed Normally.

3

Replacement

Introduction

Many systems deteriorate as time goes on unless some corrective action is taken. In some cases parts of a system fail suddenly and unpredictably, and the only corrective action possible is to replace them. Thus a labour force deteriorates as people leave, and hence replacement (recruitment and training) is necessary. A light bulb is another type of item that fails irregularly and has to be replaced. These kinds of systems will be studied first, and we shall use some of the ideas of probability that have been introduced in the previous chapter.

Some systems deteriorate gradually, leading to lower efficiency and higher costs. This is typically the case with machines that wear. For these there may also be a number of alternative policies of maintenance. Once the data about this deterioration have been collected, the time when it becomes economic to replace the system, with an associated capital cost, rather than continue to operate the old system can be calculated. An example of this kind of replacement decision is given in the second part of the chapter.

Systems that fail

Light bulbs

The classic example of this kind of replacement situation is the case of light bulbs. The system consists of a number of bulbs, each of which fail suddenly after a variable period of service at full efficiency. Although individual failures are unpredictable, the statistical characteristics of the group of bulbs are often stable. When it is cheaper per bulb to replace them as a group (even though some may not have failed yet) than to replace bulbs individually, what replacement policy should be followed?

EXAMPLE 1

Suppose that a special-purpose type of light bulb never lasts longer than 2 weeks and there is some chance that a bulb will fail at the end of the first week. There are 100 new bulbs initially, the cost per bulb of individual replacement is £1, and the cost per bulb for a group replacement is £0·50. The probability of failure at the end of the first week is 0·3. Is it cheapest to replace all bulbs (*a*) every week, (*b*) every other week, (*c*) every third week, (*d*) individually?

Solution

(*a*) Every week: Group replacement of 100 bulbs costs £50. If this is done every week, $100 \times 0·3 = 30$ failed bulbs and 70 usable ones will be replaced at the end of each week, costing £50 per week. There will be no individual replacements.

(*b*) Every 2 weeks: On average 30 bulbs will be replaced individually at the end of the first week, at a cost of £30. All bulbs will be replaced at the end of the second week, at a cost of £50. The total cost for the 2 weeks is £80 and so the average cost is £40 per week.

(*c*) Every 3 weeks: How many bulbs will have to be replaced individually at the end of the first and second weeks before group replacement takes place? 30 bulbs fail at the end of the first week and are replaced with new ones. Of these latter, $30 \times 0·3 = 9$ will fail at the end of the second week and be replaced individually; the other 21 will fail at the end of the third week and will be replaced during group replacement. There are also the original bulbs that did not fail during the first week, but will during the second week (since no bulb lasts longer than 2 weeks). There are 70 of these to be replaced individually. Of the new ones installed some will fail in the third week (their first) and will get replaced, along with all others during group replacement.

The total number of individual replacements during the first 2 weeks is, therefore:

$$30 + 9 + 70 = 109,$$

and the cost is £109. There is also the cost of the group replacement, £50, so that the total cost during the 3 weeks is 109 + 50 = £159. The average cost of this policy is therefore £53 per week.

(*d*) Individual replacement: The number of bulbs divided by the average life of a bulb is the average number of bulbs that will need to be replaced individually each week.

The average life is:

$$1 \text{ week} \times 0 \cdot 3 = 0 \cdot 3$$
$$2 \text{ weeks} \times 0 \cdot 7 = 1 \cdot 4$$

Average life $1 \cdot 7$ weeks

Therefore:

$$\frac{100}{1 \cdot 7} = 59 \text{ bulbs per week fail on average.}$$

Hence, the average cost of this policy is £59 per week.

Cheapest policy The average cost per week of each policy is:

(*a*) £50 per week   (*b*) £40 per week
(*c*) £53 per week   (*d*) £59 per week.

Of these the cheapest is (*b*), group replacement every 2 weeks and individual replacements in between.

Failure trees
In the previous example the number of individual replacements expected for various policies was calculated. Since a bulb either failed at the end of the first week with a certain probability or failed at the end of the second week, keeping track of how many bulbs fail during the course of time was relatively easy. For more complex failure patterns, however, a useful device is a failure tree.

A failure tree can be grown (conventionally from left to right in this context) period by period. Starting at the end of period 0 with 100 new bulbs, a horizontal branch represents those that do not fail at the end of the first week, a diagonal branch represents those that do. In this case the expected numbers of these are:

$$0 \cdot 7 \times 100 = 70 \text{ and } 0 \cdot 3 \times 100 = 30.$$

The tree at this stage is shown in Fig. 3.1.

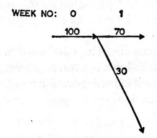

Fig. 3.1   Failure tree (Example 1) at end of first week

To extend this to the end of the second week, the 70 1-week-old bulbs all fail. Of the 30 bulbs replaced, $9 = 0.3 \times 30$ are expected to fail at the end of the first week of their life and 21 are expected to survive. Thus the tree has grown as shown in Fig. 3.2.

In Example 1 it was not necessary to extend the tree into the third period. Since all bulbs were group-replaced not later than the third week, the number of failures at the end of the third week would not be replaced individually. If a group replacement policy every 4 or more weeks was being considered, extending the failure tree could be easily done. The use of a tree of this kind, particularly for more variable failures than the 2-week pattern of Example 1, is illustrated

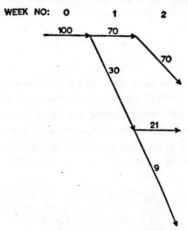

Fig. 3.2   Failure tree at end of second week

in Example 2. But before coming to this, we need to discuss survival probabilities.

Survival probabilities

Given an initial population of new bulbs, say 100, the number still in operation at the end of each week can be counted. The ratio of this to the original number is then the probability that a bulb will survive at least until the end of that week. Suppose that observation gives the following results:

Week No.	No. of bulbs in operation at end of week	Survival probability beyond week
0	100	1·0
1	90	0·9
2	60	0·6
3	20	0·2
4	0	0·0

From these survival probabilities the probability distribution of bulb life may be constructed. This is given below:

Life weeks x	Probability p	px
1	0·1	0·1
2	0·3	0·6
3	0·4	1·2
4	0·2	0·8
	——	——
	1·0	$\Sigma px = 2\cdot7$ weeks, mean life

EXAMPLE 2

Using the above distribution of life, and given that a group replacement of 100 bulbs costs £25, and that an individual replacement of 100 bulbs costs £1 per bulb, investigate alternative replacement policies. Assume now that failure occurs at random during the week (not just at the end of the week), and that these bulbs must be replaced individually at the time.

Solution

(a) Individual replacement: Since the average life of bulbs is now 0·5 weeks less, i.e. 2·2 weeks, the average cost per week of individual replacements is:

$$\frac{100}{2 \cdot 2} \times £1 = £45$$

(b) Group and some individual replacements: The number of individual replacements for a given group replacement interval can be calculated from the failure tree. In this case the probabilities are such that the tree is as in Fig. 3.3.

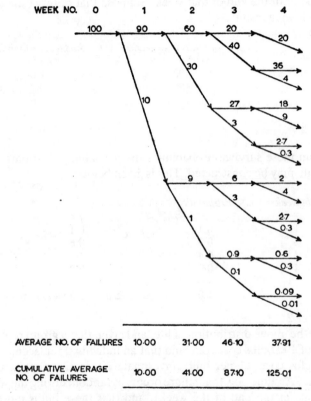

Fig. 3.3   Failure tree for Example 2

For each week the sum of numbers on each diagonal represents the average number of failures. From these the cumulative average number of individual failures in the first week, in the first 2 weeks, etc., can be calculated. Since individual replacements cost £1 per bulb, the cost of these, related to the interval between group replacements, is as follows:

Interval between group replacements (weeks)	Cost of individual replacements (£)
1	10·00
2	41·00
3	87·10
4	125·01

The cost of a group replacement is £25. Therefore the total cost and the average cost per week are:

Interval between group replacements (weeks)	Total cost (£)	Average cost per week (£)
1	35·00	35·00
2	66·00	33·00
3	112·10	37·37
4	150·01	37·50

The best of these policies is to replace all bulbs every 2 weeks and to replace individual bulbs during the 2 weeks, at an average cost of £33·00 per week.

(c) Optimal policy: The best group replacement policy costs £33 per week, and to replace only individually as required costs £45 per week. Therefore the best overall policy is the group replacement one. This happens to be the same best policy as in Example 1.

Systems that wear

Probably the most familiar example of gradual deterioration of a system is the motor-car. Though the replacement decision in practice may be taken on other than economic grounds (especially for cars), a knowledge of the cost of alternative policies is still very relevant. The situation examined here is when annual operating and maintenance costs increase as time goes on.

EXAMPLE 3

A new car costs £8000 and may be sold at the end of any year at the following prices:

Year (end)	1	2	3	4	5	6
Selling price (£)	5000	3300	2000	1100	600	100

The corresponding annual operating and maintenance costs are shown below.

Year (end)	1	2	3	4	5	6
Op. & m. cost/yr (£)	1000	1200	1500	2000	3000	5000

How often should a new car with identical characteristics be bought if the average total cost per period is to be minimised?

Solution   If the car is sold after one year, the capital cost is 8000 − 5000 = £3000, so the total cost for the year is 3000 + 1000 = £4000. If the car is sold after two years, the capital cost is 8000 − 3300 = £4700, so the total cost is 4700 + 1000 + 1200 = £6900, or an average of £3450 per year. Tabulating these with the other possibilities, we obtain:

Replacement interval (yrs)	Capital cost (£)	Total Op. & m. cost (£)	Total cost (£)	Average cost/yr (£)
1	3000	1000	4000	4000
2	4700	2200	6900	3450
3	6000	3700	9700	3233
4	6900	5700	12600	3150
5	7400	8700	16100	3220
6	7900	13700	21600	3600

Thus the average total cost per year is minimised (£3150) if the car is replaced every 4 years.

EXAMPLE 4

If it is possible not only to sell the car after use but also to buy a car second hand, it may be cheaper to do so than to replace with a new car. The additional data needed is the cost of buying a car of various ages, i.e.

Age of car (yrs)	0	1	2	3	4	5
Purchase price (£)	8000	5800	4000	2600	1600	1000

What is the age to buy and to sell the car to minimise total average costs per year?

Solution The calculation of average cost per year now has to be done in four stages:

1 The capital cost of each possible combination of age at purchase and age at sale.
2 The total operating and maintenance costs of these possibilities.
3 The sum of these two, i.e. the total cost from one replacement to the next.
4 Dividing each sum by the corresponding number of years to give the average total cost per year.

The replacement policy for which 4 is a minimum is then the best.

Each stage of the calculation can be presented as a table, relating to the age of the car at purchase and to the age of the car at sale.

1 *Capital cost* (= purchase price − selling price), £

		Age at sale (yrs)					
		1	2	3	4	5	6
	0	3000	4700	6000	6900	7400	7900
Age at	1		2500	3800	4700	5200	5700
purchase	2			2000	2900	3400	3900
(yrs)	3				1500	2000	2500
	4					1000	1500
	5						900

The first line of this table was already calculated in the previous example. The other lines use the additional figures for purchase prices of second-hand cars.

2 *Cumulative operating and maintenance costs, £*

		Age at sale (yrs)					
		1	2	3	4	5	6
	0	1000	2200	3700	5700	8700	13700
Age at	1		1200	2700	4700	7700	12700
purchase	2			1500	3500	6500	11500
(yrs)	3				2000	5000	10000
	4					3000	8000
	5						5000

The first line of this table was also calculated in the previous example. The other lines are just the sum of the relevant costs for cars acquired second hand.

3   *Total cost* from one replacement to the next, £

		1	2	3	4	5	6
				Age at sale (yrs)			
	0	4000	6900	9700	12600	16100	21600
Age at	1		3700	6500	9400	12900	18400
purchase	2			3500	6400	9900	15400
(yrs)	3				3500	7000	12500
	4					4000	9500
	5						5900

Each entry is the sum of the entry in (1) and the entry in (2) for the particular replacement policy. However, the figures in (3) correspond to replacement intervals varying between 1 year and 6 years. To compare average total cost per year, they must be divided by the replacement interval. The diagonals running in the table from NW to SE correspond to 1 year, 2 years, 3 years, etc., and the single possibility of a 6-year replacement costs £21600 or £3600 per year.

4   *Average total cost per year,* £

		1	2	3	4	5	6
				Age at sale (yrs)			
	0	4000	3450	3233	3150	3220	3600
Age at	1		3700	3250	3133	3225	3680
purchase	2			3500	3200	3300	3850
(yrs)	3				3500	3500	4166
	4					4000	4750
	5						5900

The replacement policy that minimises the average total cost per year is to buy a 1-year-old car and to sell it when it is 4 years old, i.e. after using it for 3 years. This policy costs £3133 per year. With the data used in this example, any policy of buying a car not more than 2 years old and selling it when it is between 3 and 5 years old, gives an average cost per year of less than 12% above the minimum. Thus the replacement decision would not be very critical within these limits.

The calculation of the average total cost per year has been carried out for all possible policies in this example. This would become impractical where the number of alternatives is very large, and a more selective method, such as dynamic programming, would be needed.

Criteria for replacement

The economics of systems are dependent on their design, on the required degree of robustness or reliability, and on the alternative maintenance policies available. The examples in this chapter have concentrated on reducing the average cost per period to a minimum, and problems of reliability and different maintenance policies have been ignored. In some systems, the automatic controls for aircraft landing for example, the need for reliability outweighs consideration of maintenance costs. In some mechanical systems maintenance costs are high, and it may be preferable to allow the system to deteriorate and then be replaced, rather than bear large maintenance costs. It is not unknown for maintenance, i.e. interfering with a system, actually to accelerate the loss of efficiency. In labour turnover studies there are difficulties in knowing to what extent maintenance costs (such as improving staff conditions) prevent increased replacement (recruitment) costs, and what the economic penalty is of failing to recruit a skilled man.

With the minimum average cost per period as a criterion for the optimal replacement policy, the timing of various costs during the replacement interval was ignored. Thus with an interval of 3 years, the following policies would be regarded as identical:

	A	B
1st year	600	100
2nd year	100	300
3rd year	300	600
Total cost	1000	1000
Average cost per year	$333\frac{1}{3}$	$333\frac{1}{3}$

If money not required this year can be invested until it is needed to meet expenses, these policies become different. Thus with an initial sum of £1000 at the beginning of the first year, with a rate of return from investment of 10% per annum, and with expenses being paid at the start of each year, the result is:

	A	B
Initial cash in hand	1000	1000
Expenses (1st year)	− 600	− 100
Balance for investment	400	900
Interest (1st year) 10%	+ 40	+ 90
Cash in hand	440	990
Expenses (2nd year)	− 100	− 300
Balance for investment	340	690
Interest (2nd year) 10%	+ 34	+ 69
Cash in hand	374	759
Expenses (3rd year)	− 300	− 600
Balance for investment	74	159
Interest (3rd year) 10%	+ 7·4	+ 15·9
Net balance (end of 3rd year)	81·4	174·9

Though it is not suggested that replacement would be financed in this way, this example illustrates the fact that when the time-value of money is taken into account, policy *B* is clearly preferable to policy *A*. The details of such procedures, of which discounted cash flow (DCF) is a popular example, require more space than is available here. The book by Kaufmann, referred to in the bibliography, contains relevant material. The examples earlier in this chapter can all be developed to allow for the time-value of money. The extent to which the choice of optimal policy would be different depends on the interest rate, or rate of return, that would apply.

Other criteria for replacement that are sometimes used include:

Replace when the system is worn out

This ignores economic considerations altogether, which is unlikely to be the optimal policy for large systems or when designs and technology are changing rapidly. A pseudo-economic criterion sometimes used is:

Replace when the system is fully depreciated

Depreciation, i.e. the writing-down of the value of the system over a number of years, does not represent a cash flow or actual expenditure. It may be set arbitrarily without reference to other economic costs, such as maintenance costs. A system is often regarded as 'free', once it is fully depreciated. This is an absurd idea and may lead to obsolete equipment being replaced far too late.

As with problems in other contexts, the development of the proper criterion is just as important as the calculation of the optimal policy for a given criterion. When the number of items for which operating data are accumulated is sufficiently large, a computer may be worth using for maintaining the records. Computers have also been used to investigate large numbers of alternative replacement policies in the search for an optimal policy.

Exercises

3.1 By how much must the cost per bulb of group replacement in Example 1 increase, if individual replacement is to be cheaper than any of the three group replacement policies examined?

3.2 If the cost per bulb of group replacement increases to £0·59 and £0·68, how do the three group replacement policies compare with individual replacement?

3.3 Extend the failure tree in Fig. 3.2 to the third and fourth weeks.

3.4 Calculate the probability of a staff resignation in each year from the following survival table:

Year no.	No. of original staff employed at end of year
0	1000
1	940
2	820
3	580
4	400
5	280
6	190
7	130
8	70
9	30
10	0

3.5 For a make of car that has been mass-produced for some time, investigate the second-hand prices of cars of different ages. From your own or a friend's data on the annual operating and maintenance costs, calculate the optimal replacement policy along the lines of Example 5. (Second-hand car prices may be influenced by changes in taxation provisions and by the time of year.)

4

Forecasting

Introduction

Forecasting the future demand for a product or service, like other forms of crystal-gazing, is a hazardous operation. Nevertheless, a forecast has to be available for making major investment decisions, in preparing production plans, or in replenishing stocks. The problem, therefore, is *how* to forecast, not whether to do so.

Methods of forecasting may be of the following kinds:

1 Statistical analysis of past data of the variable being forecast.
2 Statistical analysis of data of other variables which are shown to be related to the one of interest.
3 Intuition, inside information, etc.

Methods 1 and 2 depend on the assumption that there are past data, and that their statistical characteristics will remain the same at least until the next reassessment of the forecast is made. This is typically the case for individual products with modest value and reasonably large demand. As well as the forecast itself, the chances of errors of different sizes are measured, and are a significant part of the usefulness of such methods. These methods cannot, however, anticipate changes in external factors, of which government decisions might be an important example. In contrast, methods of type 3 are essential in predicting these types of changes, but they may be rather poor in dealing with large numbers of routine forecasts. Thus a combination of methods often produces the most effective way of tackling the problem of forecasting.

In reaching a decision about the particular combination of methods to be used, one has to consider questions such as:

(*a*) What has to be forecast, and why? In how much detail?
(*b*) How far into the future must it be forecast? With what accuracy?
(*c*) What methods are possible in the context?
(*d*) What information is available? How reliable is it? When is it available? How frequently is new information available?
(*e*) What are the important external factors? How can these be anticipated?
(*f*) What are the costs of establishing and operating different forecasting methods?
(*g*) What are the costs of different sizes of errors in forecasting?
(*h*) How does the forecast affect other parts of the system?

In answering such questions it is assumed that the person requiring to make the forecast does not have control over the variable to be forecast. Even so, forecasts can be self-fulfilling in some situations, so beware of the perfect forecast!

This chapter deals only with methods of type 1, and only with a few of such methods. These are particularly relevant in the context of stock control (see Chapter 5), but they also show up some of the more general problems of forecasting.

Regularity

A series of observations often appears to have some degree of regularity. This is partly obscured, however, by deviations from the strict pattern. For a given series of data, the assumption of a different form of regularity leads to a different set of deviations in the data from that regularity. One way of expressing the problem of forecasting is the question: how can one select the appropriate form of regularity (with its associated pattern of deviations) on which to base one's forecast? Before trying to answer this question, let us examine a few of the forms of regularity that may occur.

EXAMPLE 1 – No trend
The series:

$$29, 29, 29, 29, 29$$

is clearly trivial, i.e. a forecast of 29.

EXAMPLE 2 – Linear trend
The series:

$$29, 30, 31, 32, 33, 34, 35, 36$$

is almost as simple, having a constant rate of increase of 1 unit per observation, so the next value forecast is 37.

EXAMPLE 3 – Exponential growth
The series:

$$29, 58, 116, 232, 464$$

is doubling at each period. Thus the next value forecast would be 928. That this is a very rapidly increasing situation can be illustrated by the age-old chess board (8×8 squares) problem: put 1 grain of corn on the first square, 2 on the second, 4 on the third, and so on; how many are there altogether on the 64 squares? (Answer: $2^{64} - 1$, or about 18 000 000 000 000 000 000 if the squares are large enough.)

EXAMPLE 4 – Exponential decay
Series can go regularly down as well as up:

$$29, 14\tfrac{1}{2}, 7\tfrac{1}{4}, 3\tfrac{5}{8}, 1\tfrac{13}{16}$$

Here each succeeding value is half its predecessor, and at this rate the observations drop to insignificant size very quickly. The next value forecast is: $\frac{29}{32}$.

EXAMPLE 5 – Cyclical
The series:

$$29, 24, 29, 34, 29, 24, 29, 34$$

has an oscillating pattern, rather than an increasing or decreasing trend. Thus the next value forecast is 29 again. If the length of the cycle (in this case four periods) is one year, then the variation is referred to as 'seasonal', such as sales of ice cream and air-tickets. There may be cycles, however, which are not related to the seasons.

EXAMPLE 6 – Linear trend and cyclical
Combining the series in Examples 2 and 5 gives the series:

$$58, 54, 60, 66, 62, 58, 64, 70$$

The next value forecast is 66.

Obviously it is easy enough to construct data having these or many other kinds of regularities for illustrative purposes. What is much more difficult is to decide how to represent actual data by some form of regularity together with an associated set of deviations. In order to do this one has to examine the frequency distribution of such deviations or errors. The average of the distribution should be 0; otherwise we could allow for the bias, one way or another, and modify our assumption on regularity to give a better forecast. The smaller the variability in the error distribution, the more reliable will the forecast be. Thus let us examine the distribution of error.

Error distribution

Suppose that some observations fluctuated about 0 at random and were never less than -2 or more than $+2$. Then the number of times that -2 occurred, -1, 0, $+1$ and $+2$ occurred in a series of 10 observations might give the following frequencies of occurrence:

Error x	Frequency f	fx
-2	1	-2
-1	2	-2
0	4	0
$+1$	2	2
$+2$	1	2
	$\Sigma f = 10$	$\Sigma fx = 0$

This distribution has a mean error of 0. It would be possible to make a forecast of 0 for the next period, and to accept that the differences from this forecast would have the above error distribution with a standard deviation of $1 \cdot 1$. Thus a typical sequence of observations might be:

$$0, +1, 0, -2, +1, -1, 0, 0, +2, -1$$

This series of numbers might also have arisen as the differences between a linear trend forecast and actual observations, as illustrated by the next example.

EXAMPLE 7 – Linear trend with errors

The series:

$$29, 29, 31, 34, 32, 35, 35, 36, 35, 39$$

could be described approximately by the linear trend in Example 2. If this trend was used as the forecast, then the errors would be:

Forecast:	29,	30,	31,	32,	33,	34,	35,	36,	37,	38
Observed:	29,	29,	31,	34,	32,	35,	35,	36,	35,	39
Error	0,	+1,	0,	−2,	+1,	−1,	0,	0,	+2,	−1

Since the mean error is again zero, and the sign of the individual error appears to change at random, the forecast looks reasonable. If all the positive errors were towards the beginning and all the negative errors towards the end, there would be grounds for altering the basis of the forecast and getting an improvement, i.e. reduction in errors. However, the errors appear to be random and there are statistical tests available to test this more rigorously. But having done this, may there not be some other line to use as a forecast which is even better? To find the best possible line the technique of linear regression has been developed.

Linear regression

The data on which a forecast is to be made consists of a set of n pairs of figures, each of which consists of the number of the time period, x, and the value observed, y. Thus in the previous example, for $x = 1$, $y = 29$, for $x = 2$, $y = 29$, for $x = 3$, $y = 31$, and so on. A forecast is to be made for the value of y expected at a specified period, e.g. $x = 11$. The line on which the forecast is made can be written as:

$$y = mx + c$$

The forecasting problem then becomes that of selecting the best values of m and c, since knowing these and the particular x, the value of y may be calculated.

It can be shown that the best values for m and c are given by:

$$m = \frac{n \sum xy - (\sum x \sum y)}{n \sum x^2 - (\sum x)^2}$$

and

$$c = \frac{\sum y - m \sum x}{n}$$

These values are 'best' in the sense that they minimise the total of the squares of all the deviations of the observations from the value forecast by the line. If one tries only to minimise the sum of the deviations themselves (not squared), positive and negative deviations can cancel each other out exactly, even though the line chosen does not fit the data at all well. This is best shown by the next small example, before applying linear regression to the data in the last example.

EXAMPLE 8
The series of observations:

$$1, 1, 2, 2, 4$$

might be represented by the line giving forecast values of:

$$2, 2, 2, 2, 2$$

The errors of the forecast are then:

$$+1, +1, 0, 0, -2$$

Their sum is 0, and the sum of their squares is 6. But clearly a better forecast would be made with the line giving forecast values of:

$$0, 1, 2, 3, 4$$

The errors of the forecast with this line are:

$$-1, 0, 0, +1, 0$$

of which the sum is again 0 and the sum of squares is now only 2. The best forecasts of all are those from the line given by linear regression, i.e.:

x	y	x^2	xy
1	1	1	1
2	1	4	2
3	2	9	6
4	2	16	8
5	4	25	20
$\Sigma x = 15$	$\Sigma y = 10$	$\Sigma x^2 = 55$	$\Sigma xy = 37$

Now

$$m = \frac{n\,\Sigma\,xy - (\Sigma\,x\,\Sigma\,y)}{n\,\Sigma\,x^2 - (\Sigma\,x)^2}$$

$$= \frac{5(37) - (15)(10)}{5(55) - (15)^2}$$

$$= 0\cdot 7$$

and

$$c = \frac{\Sigma\,y - m\,\Sigma\,x}{n}$$

$$= \frac{10 - 0\cdot 7 \times 15}{5}$$

$$= -0\cdot 1$$

Therefore, comparing the best forecasts from

$$y = 0\cdot 7x - 0\cdot 1$$

with the actual observations:

	Forecast	*Observation*	*Error*	*Error^2*
x	*y*			
1	0·6	1	−0·4	0·16
2	1·3	1	+0·3	0·09
3	2·0	2	0·0	0·00
4	2·7	2	+0·7	0·49
5	3·4	4	−0·6	0·36
			0·0	1·10

Thus the forecast with $y = 0\cdot 7x - 0\cdot 1$ gives not only a sum of errors equal to 0 but the sum of (error^2) as small as possible (1·1 in this case). No other straight line can reduce this further.

Having shown how to use linear regression to fit the best linear trend to a series of n observations, let us investigate how this technique would have fitted the best line to the data given in Example 7.

EXAMPLE 9 – Linear regression on the data of Example 7

x	y	x^2	xy
1	29	1	29
2	29	4	58
3	31	9	93
4	34	16	136
5	32	25	160
6	35	36	210
7	35	49	245
8	36	64	288
9	35	81	315
10	39	100	390
$\Sigma x = 55$	$\Sigma y = 335$	$\Sigma x^2 = 385$	$\Sigma xy = 1924$

Hence

$$m = \frac{n\Sigma xy - (\Sigma x \Sigma y)}{n \Sigma x^2 - (\Sigma x)^2}$$

$$= \frac{10(1924) - (55)(335)}{10(385) - (55)^2}$$

$$= 1$$

and

$$c = \frac{\Sigma y - m \Sigma x}{n}$$

$$= \frac{335 - 1 \times 55}{10}$$

$$= 28$$

Thus the best forecast line is:

$$y = x + 28$$

and the comparison, between the observations themselves and the forecast is:

x	Forecast *y*	Observation	Error	Error^2
1	29	29	0	0
2	30	29	+1	1
3	31	31	0	0
4	32	34	−2	4
5	33	32	+1	1
6	34	35	−1	1
7	35	35	0	0
8	36	36	0	0
9	37	35	+2	4
10	38	39	−1	1
			0	12

Thus, if we want to use a straight line as a basis for forecasting the next value (the 11th), this would be:

$$y = 11 + 28 = 39$$

That this forecast gives the same linear trend as that of Example 2, and has the same error distribution as that given earlier, is a result of the data having been constructed to illustrate these very points.

In these examples linear regression has been used when the variable x is time. The variable y might have been the number of items sold in each time period. This is rather a special case and may require additional analysis to linear regression. A more general application of linear regression would be when x is, for example, the number of inches of rainfall or the score achieved by salesmen on an intelligence test. Linear regression can also be extended to relate y to a number of x variables simultaneously. The calculations involved can usually be carried out using a standard computer program.

Adaptive forecasting

Returning to the practical problem of analysing a series of observations, obviously there is the question whether to fit a line, or a cyclical function, or both, or some other form of regularity. This can be tackled by statistical techniques of curve fitting, of which linear regression is the simplest. Further references to these are given in the bibliography. But all of these are of a once-for-all nature. This may be the situation where a major research effort is needed to collect the data, and where a forecast is only needed once.

Many manufacturing operations involve items that may be in continuous, though fluctuating, demand. Weekly sales data, for example, may be collected on a routine basis, and one wants to revise the sales forecasts in the light of the latest information. In this situation one needs a method of forecasting that is adaptive, i.e. one that is easy to revise and in doing so corrects for earlier differences between a forecast and the actual volume of sales. Though one could use linear regression each time a new observation became available, either on all the data or probably on the latest n observations, this would not be very satisfactory. An easier method would be to use a moving average, or even simpler, a method such as exponential smoothing. These two methods of forecasting are considered in the paragraphs that follow.

Moving average

A moving average is calculated simply by adding up the last n observations and dividing by n. When the next observation becomes available, the oldest observation in the earlier calculation is dropped, the new one is added in and a new average calculated.

EXAMPLE 10 – Moving average on the data of Example 7
The series of observations was:

$$29, 29, 31, 34, 32, 35, 35, 36, 35, 39$$

If one chose to calculate the moving average on 3 observations, the sequence of calculations would be:

$$(29 + 29 + 31)/3 = 29\tfrac{2}{3}$$
$$(29 + 31 + 34)/3 = 31\tfrac{1}{3}$$
$$(31 + 34 + 32)/3 = 32\tfrac{1}{3}$$
$$(34 + 32 + 35)/3 = 33\tfrac{2}{3}$$
$$(32 + 35 + 35)/3 = 34$$
$$(35 + 35 + 36)/3 = 35\tfrac{1}{3}$$
$$(35 + 36 + 35)/3 = 35\tfrac{1}{3}$$
$$(36 + 35 + 39)/3 = 36\tfrac{2}{3}$$

This moving average increases steadily for this particular data and value of n, so that it smooths out most of the fluctuations in the data. However, it does lag behind the data when there is linear trend. This may be shown by comparing the moving average of 3 observations with the actual observation 1 period later:

Moving av.	Observation	Moving av. – Obs.
$29\frac{2}{3}$	34	$-4\frac{1}{3}$
$31\frac{1}{3}$	32	$-\frac{2}{3}$
$32\frac{1}{3}$	35	$-2\frac{2}{3}$
$33\frac{2}{3}$	35	$-1\frac{1}{3}$
34	36	-2
$35\frac{1}{3}$	35	$+\frac{1}{3}$
$35\frac{1}{3}$	39	$-3\frac{2}{3}$
$36\frac{2}{3}$		

EXAMPLE 11 – Moving average on the data of Example 5
The series was cyclical, i.e.

$$29, 24, 29, 34, 29, 24, 29, 34$$

Clearly, if a moving average of 4 observations (the length of the cycle) is calculated, then it will remain at the value of 29 for as long as this regular cycle persists. But suppose that the cycle length was not so obvious, and a moving average of 2, or of 3, observations had been selected as shown below.

Moving av. (2)	Moving av. (3)	Observation
$26\frac{1}{2}$	–	29
$26\frac{1}{2}$	$27\frac{1}{3}$	34
$31\frac{1}{2}$	29	29
$31\frac{1}{2}$	$30\frac{2}{3}$	24
$26\frac{1}{2}$	29	29
$26\frac{1}{2}$	$27\frac{1}{3}$	34

When a moving average of 2 is taken, the result is a 'battlement', i.e. it jumps between $26\frac{1}{2}$ and $31\frac{1}{2}$ every other time. Though the range, 5, is less than that of the original observations, 10, the moving average is at a high value when the actual observation is at its lowest, and vice versa.

When a moving average of 3 is taken, the range of the fluctuation in the moving average is smaller, $3\frac{1}{3}$, and the moving average is at 29 every time the observation is at 29. But the moving average rises above 29 just when the observation goes below 29, and vice versa.

The data used in this example are much more regular than many real life data, and exaggerate the effect of different values of n. Obviously with such regular cycles one can predict the next value exactly, without calculating a moving average of any length. But the example illustrates some of the potential difficulties in using moving averages.

The moving average method means that a list of n individual observations has to be kept, which for large n is rather laborious. How big should n be? If n is large, the moving average will give a forecast that changes only slowly. If the variation in the data is not just random, however, but follows a trend, the moving average will be slow to take account of this. Alternatively, if n is small, the moving average is more sensitive to change. But this means that it will vary rather more also when the data are affected simply by random fluctuations. So a balance has to be achieved between *stability* of the forecast given random variation and *sensitivity* of the forecast given a change in trend. The question of this balance arises in any adaptive forecasting method; the form it takes for the moving average method is the number of observations, n, to include in the moving average. The balance to adopt is determined by the values (or costs) attached to varying degrees of stability and of sensitivity in a particular context.

Exponential smoothing

This cumbersome title (which will be explained later) conceals an adaptive forecasting technique of great simplicity. Suppose that a new observation has just been made, and that we already have an old forecast, based on any method we like. There will almost certainly be a difference between the forecast and the actual observation. Therefore let us construct our forecast of the *next* observation from our old one by allowing for the error we have just made. We shall overcompensate if we change our forecast by the full extent of the error, since some of it will be due to random fluctuations in the observations. The correction should be just some fraction of the error. This method can then be written:

new forecast = old forecast + α(latest observation – old forecast)

where α (alpha) is a fraction between 0 and 1. The error in our old forecast is (latest observation – old forecast). Once we have decided what value the fraction α should have, it is kept constant, and a new forecast can be calculated very quickly as soon as the latest observation becomes available. Notice how α affects the stability and sensitivity of the forecast. If α equals 0, the new forecast is always the same as the old forecast, regardless of all the latest observations. Therefore once an initial forecast is made, it remains unaltered for ever after; the ultimate in stability. If α equals 1, at the other extreme, then the equation can be simplified to:

new forecast = latest observation

Thus the forecast is as variable as the observations themselves are and is always one period late. This is the ultimate in sensitivity. The actual value of α determines the balance between sensitivity and stability, and it has been found appropriate to have α between 0·1 and 0·2 in many systems. α is called 'the smoothing constant'.

The amount of information that has to be stored when forecasting by exponential smoothing is very small: the old forecast, the value of α, and the latest observation. This has led to its widespread use in computerised systems. But why exponential?

Let

F_0 be the new forecast for the next period
F_1 ,, ,, forecast made 1 period ago for the present period
F_2 ,, ,, ,, ,, 2 periods ago for the next period
F_3 ,, ,, ,, ,, 3 ,, ,, ,, ,, ,, ,,
F_4 ,, ,, ,, ,, 4 ,, ,, ,, ,, ,, ,,

and so on.

Also, let

D_1 be the latest observation (for the present period)
D_2 ,, ,, previous ,, (1 period ago)
D_3 ,, ,, ,, ,, (2 periods ,,)
D_4 ,, ,, ,, ,, (3 ,, ,,)

and so on.

We can write the new forecast in the form:

$$F_0 = F_1 + \alpha(D_1 - F_1)$$

or

$$F_0 = \alpha D_1 + (1 - \alpha)F_1$$

But F_1 itself was determined in the same way as F_0, i.e. from the expression:

$$F_1 = \alpha D_2 + (1 - \alpha)F_2$$

So F_0 can be rewritten as:

$$F_0 = \alpha D_1 + (1 - \alpha)\{\alpha D_2 + (1 - \alpha)F_2\}$$

or

$$F_0 = \alpha D_1 + \alpha(1 - \alpha)D_2 + (1 - \alpha)^2 F_2$$

But the same argument applies to F_2 as it did to F_1, namely:

$$F_2 = \alpha D_3 + (1 - \alpha)F_3$$

Therefore F_0 can be written as:

$$F_0 = \alpha D_1 + \alpha(1 - \alpha)D_2 + (1 - \alpha)^2(\alpha D_3 + (1 - \alpha)F_3)$$

or

$$F_0 = \alpha D_1 + \alpha(1 - \alpha)D_2 + \alpha(1 - \alpha)^2 D_3 + (1 - \alpha)^3 F_3$$

The argument can be applied again and again indefinitely, and would produce an equation for F_0 of the form:

$$F_0 = \alpha\{D_1 + (1 - \alpha)D_2 + (1 - \alpha)^2 D_3 + (1 - \alpha)^3 D_4 \\ + (1 - \alpha)^4 D_5 + \ldots + (1 - \alpha)^k D_{k+1} + \ldots\}$$

Thus by actually calculating the new forecast in the very simple way described at the beginning of this section, it turns out that the new forecast is a weighted average of all previous observations. But the weights attached to each observation are not the same; they decrease by the fraction $(1 - \alpha)$, as observations become more remote. It is because the weights attached to the successively older observations decrease by this constant factor that the method is referred to as 'exponential' smoothing. (The proof that the sum of all the coefficients is exactly equal to 1, so that F_0 is indeed a weighted average of all past data, is set as an exercise at the end of the chapter.) Table 4.1 shows the relative weights that are implied by the forecast, F_0, for the values of $\alpha = 0\cdot05, 0\cdot1, 0\cdot2$ and $0\cdot5$.

Table 4.1 Exponential relative weights

	$\alpha = 0.05$	0.10	0.20	0.50
D_1	0.050	0.100	0.200	0.500
D_2	0.047	0.090	0.160	0.250
D_3	0.045	0.081	0.128	0.125
D_4	0.043	0.073	0.102	0.062
D_5	0.041	0.066	0.082	0.031
D_6	0.039	0.059	0.066	0.016
D_7	0.037	0.053	0.052	0.008
D_8	0.035	0.048	0.042	0.004
D_9	0.033	0.043	0.034	0.002
D_{10}	0.031	0.039	0.027	0.001
Total	0.401	0.652	0.893	0.999
$D_{>10}$	0.599	0.348	0.107	0.001
Total relative weight	1.000	1.000	1.000	1.000

Table 4.1 is only included to indicate how the forecast, F_0, is dependent on past observations in different ways for various values of α. This table would never be used to calculate F_0, since this is always done much more easily from the original statement, i.e.:

new forecast = old forecast + α(latest observation – old forecast)

or $\qquad F_0 = F_1 + \alpha(D_1 - F_1)$

EXAMPLE 12 – Exponential smoothing of constant + random fluctuations

Given an old forecast of 35 initially, compare the difference between $\alpha = \frac{1}{2}$ and $\alpha = \frac{1}{10}$, for the following series of 10 observations:

$$39, 39, 32, 37, 34, 33, 38, 34, 39, 31$$

Solution The initial forecast is 35 and the corresponding actual observation is 39. Thus, for $\alpha = \frac{1}{2}$, the forecast for the next period is:

$$= 35 + \tfrac{1}{2}(39 - 35) = 37$$

A period later, for which 37 is forecast, the observation is (the second) 39, so the new forecast then becomes:

$$= 37 + \tfrac{1}{2}(39 - 37) = 38$$

The calculation can be carried through the 10 stages for which there are data, and tabulated:

Observation	Forecast	Error	$\frac{1}{2}$ Error	New forecast
39	35	+4	+2	37
39	37	+2	+1	38
32	38	−6	−3	35
37	35	+2	+1	36
34	36	−2	−1	35
33	35	−2	−1	34
38	34	+4	+2	36
34	36	−2	−1	35
39	35	+4	+2	37
31	37	−6	−3	34
.	34			
.				
.				

The corresponding figures if the value $\alpha = \frac{1}{10}$ is used are:

Observation	Forecast	Error	$\frac{1}{10}$ Error	New forecast
39	35·0	+4·0	+0·4	35·4
39	35·4	+3·6	+0·4	35·8
32	35·8	−3·8	−0·4	35·4
37	35·4	+1·6	+0·2	35·6
34	35·6	−1·6	−0·2	35·4
33	35·4	−2·4	−0·2	35·2
38	35·2	+2·8	+0·3	35·5
34	35·5	−1·5	−0·1	35·4
39	35·4	+3·6	+0·4	35·8
31	35·8	−4·8	−0·5	35·3
.	35·3			
.				
.				

The smaller value of α produces a smoother forecast than the larger. Indeed $\alpha = \frac{1}{2}$ is an unusually large value to have in practice. The sum of the individual errors is −2 for $\alpha = \frac{1}{2}$ and +1·5 for $\alpha = \frac{1}{10}$, so that no serious bias in the forecast has developed. It is left to the exercises given at the end of the chapter for the reader to show that the method does not develop a bias when there is a sudden isolated high value (a 'pulse') in otherwise uniform data, or when there is a sudden change in the data from one uniform level to another (a 'step'). In both cases the forecast, having detected the situation, will reach the level of the observations again after a number of periods that depends on α. But a more serious situation develops when the data with no linear trend start to have one. To illustrate this, Example 13 concerns data that have a linear trend as well as random fluctuations.

EXAMPLE 13 – Exponential smoothing of linear trend + random fluctuations
Given an old forecast of 35 initially, and using $\alpha = \frac{1}{10}$, exponentially smooth the following observations:

$$41, 43, 38, 45, 44, 45, 52, 50, 57, 51$$

Solution   Setting up the 10 stages on which there are data as in Example 12, we obtain:

Observation	Forecast	Error	$\frac{1}{10}$ Error	New forecast
41	35·0	+6·0	+0·6	35·6
43	35·6	+7·4	+0·7	36·3
38	36·3	+1·7	+0·2	36·5
45	36·5	+8·5	+0·9	37·4
44	37·4	+6·6	+0·7	38·1
45	38·1	+6·9	+0·7	38·8
52	38·8	+13·2	+1·3	40·1
50	40·1	+9·9	+1·0	41·1
57	41·1	+15·9	+1·6	42·7
51	42·7	+8·3	+0·8	43·5
.	43·5			
.				
.				

In this case the sum of the individual errors is +84·4, and there is obviously something wrong with such a seriously biased forecast which has underestimated on every occasion, twice to the extent of more than 10. Since the average rate of increase in the forecast is at this stage about +0·9, it may appear doubtful whether the forecast will ever catch up with the observations.

This situation arises because the data were constructed to include a linear trend of +2 per period by adding 2 to the first observation in Example 12, +4 to the second, +6 to the third, and so on. The data in Example 14 do not include any random fluctuations in order to show up more clearly how to measure this bias.

EXAMPLE 14 – Linear trend, no random fluctuations

Given an old forecast of 10, a linear trend of +2 per period, and using $\alpha = \frac{1}{2}$, exponentially smooth the observations.

Solution

Observation	Forecast	Error	$\frac{1}{2}$ Error	New forecast
12	10	+2	+1	+11
14	11	+3	$+1\frac{1}{2}$	$+12\frac{1}{2}$
16	$12\frac{1}{2}$	$+3\frac{1}{2}$	$+1\frac{3}{4}$	$+14\frac{1}{4}$
18	$14\frac{1}{4}$	$+3\frac{3}{4}$	$+1\frac{7}{8}$	$+16\frac{1}{8}$
20	$16\frac{1}{8}$	$+3\frac{7}{8}$	$+1\frac{15}{16}$	$+18\frac{1}{16}$
22	$18\frac{1}{16}$	$+3\frac{15}{16}$	$+1\frac{31}{32}$	$+20\frac{1}{32}$
.	$20\frac{1}{32}$			
.				
.				

The new forecast is calculated, row by row, in the usual way. Clearly in this case the forecast tends to be almost 4 below the corresponding observation, and it reaches the same value as the observation was 2 periods earlier.

In normal data, however, there will be random fluctuations and also a varying amount of trend. Thus the trend can only be estimated approximately. One way of forecasting the present linear trend would be by exponential smoothing, just as convenient for trend as for individual observations. The new estimate of trend would then be used to calculate the necessary correction. This would be added to the basic exponential smoothing equation to get the final forecast.

Exercises

4.1 Find by linear regression the line of best fit to the following data:

x	y
1·9	2·2
2·5	2·3
0·8	1·3
1·9	1·8
1·2	2·0
2·7	2·7
1·4	1·6

Hence forecast the value of *y* that corresponds to a value of $x = 1.6$.

4.2 Calculate the mean and standard deviation of the error distribution:

Error	Probability
−1	0·6
0	0·1
+1	0·1
+2	0·1
+3	0·1
	1·0

4.3 Given the cyclical data in Example 5 (29, 24, 29, 34, etc.), calculate the 5- and 6-period moving averages.

4.4 Prove that the sum of the exponential coefficients in:

$$F_0 = \alpha D_1 + \alpha(1 - \alpha)D_2 + \alpha(1 - \alpha)^2 D_3 + \alpha(1 - \alpha)^3 D_4 + \ldots \qquad \text{equals 1.}$$

4.5 Exponentially smooth, with $\alpha = 0.2$, the following data:

$$30, 35, 30, 30, 30, 30, 30, 30, 30$$

4.6 Exponentially smooth, with $\alpha = 0.2$, the data:

$$30, 30, 30, 35, 35, 35, 35, 35, 35$$

5

Stock Control

Introduction

Before shopping for food a person will check on what is left in the cupboard. In deciding to buy coffee but not tea he or she will have made an assessment of the time which will elapse before the next visit to the shops, together with the rate at which the tea and coffee are used. The tea may last till the next shopping day whereas the coffee may not. Possibly the amount of coffee in the larder may also be sufficient to last that long, but it may be preferred not to allow stocks to fall too low in case of an emergency.

This illustration typifies the logic of stock replenishment. In the above situation the reasoning is probably subconscious. In business situations, however, stock control certainly demands, at the very least, a conscious effort.

The two principal functions of stock are:

(*a*) to enable the product to be produced or procured in economic quantities; and

(*b*) to act as a buffer against an unpredictably high rate of use.

Stocks perform these and certain other functions at a price. This price is the cost of holding stock. The object of stock control is to ensure a correct balance between the costs of stock-holding and the benefits from stock-holding.

Economic batch quantities

Consider the first of the two functions of stock. What do we mean by an economic quantity? There are certain advantages to be gained from buying goods in large quantities. There are economies to be derived in terms of ordering, handling and transportation. There may also be savings in terms of quantity discounts. On the other hand, there are the costs – often larger than are generally recognised – of holding stocks. It is possible to make the size of batch so large that further economies are more than offset by the costs of stock-holding, especially when these costs take into account the risk of deterioration and obsolescence. A compromise is sought between too small and too large a batch. That compromise which minimises the total costs involved is called the *economic batch quantity* (EBQ).

The total cost of stock-holding is made up of several parts, e.g. capital cost and upkeep of warehouse, handling charges, deterioration, insurance, etc. By far the most important portion of the cost, however, is one which does not appear in a balance sheet. It is the interest which capital tied up in stocks could earn if invested either in the current enterprise or elsewhere, and is proportional to the value of the stock held. Many of the components of the stock-holding cost are approximately proportional to the stock value, and hence we shall assume that the annual stock-holding cost is some fraction of the average stock value. The concept of an economic batch quantity is illustrated in the following example.

EXAMPLE 1
A merchant has a steady demand for a product of 50 items per month. He buys from a supplier at a cost of £60 per item and the cost of ordering and receiving delivery of a replenishment order is £100 per occasion. If the stock-holding costs are 20% per annum of stock value, how frequently should the merchant replenish his stock?

Solution   Implied in this example are the following assumptions:

  (*a*) The demand rate is constant.
  (*b*) The time between placing a replenishment order and receiving the items into stock – called the *lead time* – is zero.
  (*c*) No stock-outs are allowed.

When the demand rate is constant and the lead time is zero it is unnecessary to hold a buffer stock for contingencies, for, by definition, these do not arise. Thus the stock should be replenished immediately (but not before) it falls to zero. The amount of stock on hand will vary between zero (immediately before a replenishment arrives) and the batch size (immediately after a replenishment) as in Fig. 5.1 and the average stock will equal half the batch size.

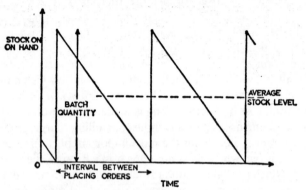

Fig. 5.1   Variation of stock level in Example 1

The stock-holding cost is 20% p.a. of the stock value. An item costs £60 and so the annual stock-holding cost is £12 × the average stock.

The annual delivery charge is £100 × the number of deliveries per year.

We may observe how the annual delivery and stock-holding costs vary with the size of batch by considering three ordering frequencies as follows:

Table 5.1   Comparison of the sums of the annual costs of stock-holding and delivery for different batch sizes

Ordering frequency	Batch size	Average stock	Stock-holding cost p.a.	Delivery cost p.a.	Stock-holding plus delivery cost p.a.
2 per month	25	$12\frac{1}{2}$	£150	£2400	£2550
8 per year	75	$37\frac{1}{2}$	£450	£800	£1250
2 per year	300	150	£1800	£200	£2000

Fig. 5.2 shows graphically how the delivery and stock-holding costs depend on the batch size.

The merchant's total annual costs comprise the annual cost of the items, the stock-holding cost and the delivery cost. The annual cost of the items does not depend on the batch size: the annual demand is 600 items, the cost price is £60 per item, and therefore the annual cost of the items is £36 000. The total annual cost, for any batch size, is £36 000 plus the appropriate value for the stock-holding and delivery cost, which may be read from Fig. 5.2. The batch size which leads to the minimum total cost is the economic batch quantity (EBQ). This is 100 items and the corresponding total annual cost is £36 000 + £1200 or £37 200.

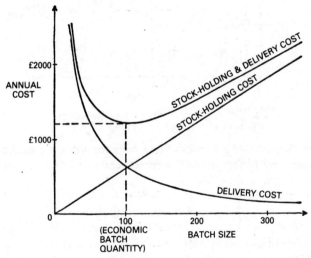

Fig. 5.2 Variation of stock-holding and delivery cost with batch size

Derivation of the economic batch quantity

The EBQ may be derived as follows:

Let d = annual demand for product
   Q = size of batch
and t = time interval between replenishment orders (years).

The above are related by the equation $t = \dfrac{Q}{d}$ and, as observed previously, the average stock is $\frac{Q}{2}$.

If we let p = cost price per item

and i = stock-holding cost p.a. (expressed as a fraction of stock value)

the stock-holding cost per item per annum = ip

and   the total annual stock-holding cost = $\frac{ipQ}{2}$

The number of deliveries per annum = $\frac{d}{Q}$

so if c = delivery cost per batch,

the annual delivery cost = $\frac{cd}{Q}$

Therefore

the total variable cost
(stock-holding + delivery) = $\frac{ipQ}{2} + \frac{cd}{Q}$

The batch size which makes this total variable cost a minimum is obtained by differentiating with respect to Q and equating the derivative to zero as follows:

$$\frac{d}{dQ} \text{ (total variable cost)} = \frac{ip}{2} - \frac{cd}{Q^2}$$

Equating this to zero yields

$$\frac{ip}{2} = \frac{cd}{Q^2} \text{ or } Q = \sqrt{\frac{2cd}{ip}}$$

Substituting the values of d, p, i and c from Example 1, we obtain the economic batch quantity

$$Q = \sqrt{\frac{2 \times 100 \times 600}{0 \cdot 2 \times 60}} = 100$$

This confirms the value from Fig. 5.2.

Quantity discounts

The derivation of the EBQ assumes a constant cost price per item, the only variable costs being the stock-holding and delivery costs. However, it may be that a reduction in the cost price can be obtained if the items are bought in large enough quantities. Example 2 illustrates the reasoning necessary to decide whether or not a price reduction more than compensates for the additional stock-holding cost.

EXAMPLE 2

In the problem of Example 1, the supplier offers a 5% discount on orders of between 200 and 999 items, and a 10% discount on orders of 1000 or more. Can the merchant reduce his costs by taking advantage of either of these discounts?

Solution   The EBQ (without discount) is 100 items. The effect of quantity discounts is to produce discontinuities in the total annual cost depending on the batch size. Fig. 5.3 shows how, in the presence of quantity discounts, the total annual cost depends on the batch size.

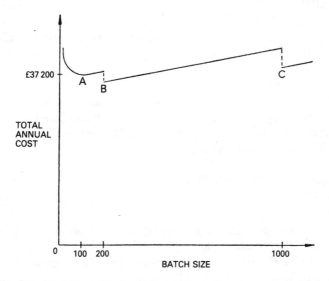

Fig. 5.3   Variation of cost with batch size in the presence of quantity discounts

In order to see whether or not a quantity discount is worth accepting, the total costs involved in purchasing the minimum sizes of batch necessary to earn the discounts (points *B* and *C* of Figure 5.3) must be compared with the cost corresponding to the EBQ (point *A*).

In taking advantage of a discount there are two sources of savings. The main saving is, of course, the lower price. A second saving, however, is that, as fewer deliveries are required, the delivery costs are reduced. On the other hand, there is the increased cost of stock-holding. A discount is only worth accepting if the savings more than offset the increased cost.

Batch size 200, discount 5%

Savings:

1   A 5% discount is a reduction of £3 per item. The annual saving due to the lower price is 600 × £3   = £1800
2   Three fewer deliveries are required per year. Each delivery costs £100 and therefore this saving is 3 × £100   = £ 300

Total annual saving = £2100

Increased cost:

The average stock is increased from 50 to 100 units whilst the annual stock-holding cost per item is reduced from £12 to 95% of this. New stock-holding cost minus old stock-holding cost is

$£(100 \times 12 \times 0.95) - £(50 \times 12)$ = £ 540

The savings outweigh the increased cost by £1560 and so the 5% discount is worth accepting.

By similar reasoning we may consider the 10% discount.

Batch size 1000, discount 10%

Savings:

1	Lower price, 600 × £6	= £3600
2	Less frequent deliveries, 5·4 × £100	= £ 540

Total annual saving = £4140

Increased cost:

New stock-holding cost minus old stock-holding

cost is £(500 × 12 × 0·9) − £(50 × 12) = £4800

The increased cost now outweighs the savings and so the 10% discount is not worth accepting. The economic batch quantity in the presence of the quantity discounts is therefore 200 items, or four months' supply.

A similar problem to that of Example 1 occurs when the stock-holder is both producer and stockist of the product. This is the case, for instance, when a manufacturing company supplies customers from a finished product stock. In this case the ordering and delivery cost is replaced by a cost of setting up machinery to make the product. The only difference between the two situations is that, whilst in the former problem replenishment of stock is instantaneous, in the latter case stock is replenished continuously over a period of time. Some of the batch may be sold whilst the remainder is still being produced. For the same size of batch, therefore, the average amount of stock on hand is less than is the case when replenishment is instantaneous. Fig. 5.4 shows how the stock on hand varies in this situation.

AC represents the interval between starting to make successive batches of the product. This is identical to *t* in the derivation of the EBQ given earlier. Retaining the same symbols as before,

$$t = \frac{Q}{d}.$$

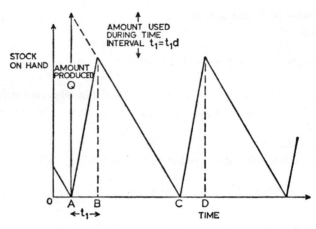

Fig. 5.4 Variation of finished stock level when stock is produced in batches

AB and CD – which are equal intervals of time, t_1 – represent the periods during which the product is actually being produced. The maximum stock occurs at the instant production ceases. The stock equals the amount produced Q minus the amount used up during the time interval t_1. This maximum stock is therefore $Q - t_1 d$.

If we let r = production rate (measured in the same units as the demand rate d), then as t_1 is the time to produce a quantity Q,

$$t_1 = \frac{Q}{r}$$

Substituting this value of t_1 in the expression for the maximum stock above,

$$\text{maximum stock} \quad = Q - \frac{dQ}{r} = Q\left(1 - \frac{d}{r}\right)$$

$$\therefore \text{ average stock} \quad = \frac{Q}{2}\left(1 - \frac{d}{r}\right)$$

The derivation of the economic batch quantity when production is not instantaneous is similar to the earlier derivation of the EBQ with the exception of the slightly modified average stock.

If we re-define c as the set-up cost per batch, the total variable cost (stock-holding + set-up)

$$= \frac{ipQ}{2}\left(1 - \frac{d}{r}\right) + \frac{cd}{Q}$$

Differentiating with respect to Q, and equating the derivative to zero for a minimum value, we find that the new economic batch quantity

$$Q = \sqrt{\frac{2cd}{ip\left(1 - \frac{d}{r}\right)}} \ .$$

The influence of uncertainty

Having analysed a stock-holding system where demand is constant and replenishment starts instantaneously, we now examine the complications which arise and the modifications necessary when such assumptions are not justified. A time lag between placing a replenishment order and receipt of goods ordered – the *lead time* – is of itself no problem so long as its duration is predictable. If the demand rate is constant, the amount of stock that will be used up during the replenishment lead time is easily calculated and the replenishment order can be initiated sufficiently far in advance to ensure that the receipt of the order coincides with the stock falling to zero. Similarly, if the lead time is zero, the fact that demand is unpredictable causes no concern. There is obviously no necessity to run out of stock when replenishment can be effected immediately. Stock control problems are caused by a combination of a demand which is unpredictable and a lead time which is greater than zero.

There are two basic types of stock control system. In the first type stock is replenished whenever the amount in stock falls to some predetermined level. This is called a '*two-bin*' or *re-order level* system. The title 'two-bin' comes from the earliest method of administering this system, which involved physically segregating the stock into two bins. Stock was drawn from the first bin until this was emptied, at which time a replenishment order was placed. Stock was then drawn from the second bin until the replenishment order arrived. When the replenishment order reached the store, the second bin was topped-up and the remainder of the stock placed into the first bin from where it was drawn again. In many stock control situations, for example a machine shop stores, this is an extremely simple system to operate.

The second method of stock control is the *periodic review system*. Under this system orders for replenishment of stock are placed at regular intervals – the quantity ordered being calculated to bring the amount in stock to some pre-determined level. This latter system is particularly useful when a range of stock items is ordered from a single supplier. Economies in order placing, and in the form of quantity discounts, may be realised by reviewing the stocks of all items in the range at the same time.

Whichever type of stock control system is used, two questions need to be answered:

(*a*) When should stock replenishment orders be placed?

(*b*) How much should be ordered when a replenishment is necessary?

We shall illustrate how these questions are answered in relation to both types of stock control system mentioned above.

The re-order level system

Earlier, in Example 1, we considered a simple stock-holding situation. Since the demand rate was constant, we could consider this either as a two-bin system – a replenishment order being placed whenever the stock falls to zero – or as a periodic review system – a replenishment occurring every 2 months. Only when the demand rate is constant, however, are the two types of system equivalent. In practice the demand rate is usually variable and there is a delay, possibly also variable, between placing and receiving a replenishment order. This gives rise to the need for safety stocks. The greater the degree of variability present, the larger is the safety stock required. How the size of the safety stock is determined in a re-order level system is illustrated in the following example.

EXAMPLE 3

The demand for a warehouse item follows a Poisson distribution with a mean of 6 per week. The value of an item is £200 and an ordering cost of £20 is incurred each time a stock replenishment order is placed. The replenishment lead time is one week. Should there be a request for an item when none is in stock, the request is met by a special delivery to the customer as soon as the next replenishment order arrives. The cost of this action is £40 per item. If the cost of stock-holding is 15% per annum of stock value, how low should stock be allowed to fall before a replenishment order is placed and how much should be ordered when a replenishment is necessary?

Solution The procedure for determining the economic batch quantity is identical to that outlined earlier. Using the same notation,

d = 6 per week, i.e. 300 per year (assuming 50 weeks per year)
p = £200 per item
i = 0·15 p.a.
c = £20

$$Q = \sqrt{\frac{2dc}{ip}} = \sqrt{\frac{2 \times 300 \times 20}{0 \cdot 15 \times 200}} = 20$$

The economic batch quantity is 20 items. This answers the question of how much should be ordered when a replenishment is necessary.

The second question to be answered is: how low should stock be allowed to fall before a replenishment order for 20 items is placed? If the demand rate were constant, a replenishment order would be placed whenever the stock fell to 6 items – this being the number required during the replenishment lead time. There would be no fluctuations to guard against and therefore no safety stock. Because the demand rate varies, however, we cannot predict how many items will be required during the replenishment lead time. We do know from the demand distribution that there will be many occasions when more than 6 items will be required, and therefore it will be necessary to place replenishment orders before the stock falls to 6 units. Stock held in excess of 6 units when a replenishment order is placed is called safety stock. Fig. 5.5 shows how the stock level varies in this example.

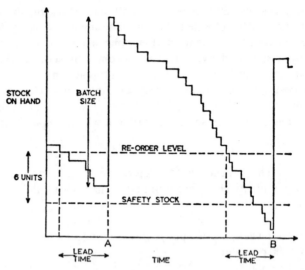

Fig. 5.5 Variation of stock level in a two-bin system

During the first lead time (Fig. 5.5) less than 6 items are required, whereas the requirement during the second lead time is more than 6. This results in the stock being higher than the safety stock at point *A* but lower than the safety stock at point *B*. When the number of items required during the lead time exceeds the safety stock plus 6 units, the excess demand cannot be supplied until the replenishment order arrives. This situation is called a *stock-out*. The higher the safety stock, the smaller is the risk of a stock-out, and vice-versa. A compromise is sought between unnecessarily high costs of stock-holding and too frequent stock-outs. (This is a similar compromise to that which obtains in determining the EBQ.) The optimum level of safety stock is that level for which the sum of the annual costs of stock-holding and stock-out is a minimum. This optimum level will be found by computing these costs for all possible levels of safety stock.

(*a*) Stock-holding cost: the expected annual cost of carrying a safety stock of *x* units is simply ipx.

(*b*) Stock-out cost: the expected number of stock-outs per lead time is a weighted average of all the possible magnitudes of stock-out, each level of stock-out being weighted by its probability of occurrence. For example, if the safety stock is 2 units, a stock-out will occur whenever the demand in the replenishment lead time exceeds 8 units. The average number of stock-outs per lead time is:

$1 \times$ (probability that the demand is   9)
$+2 \times$ (,,   ,,   ,,   ,,   ,, 10)
$+3 \times$ (,,   ,,   ,,   ,,   ,, 11)
$+4 \times$ (,,   ,,   ,,   ,,   ,, 12)
$+5 \times$ (,,   ,,   ,,   ,,   ,, 13)

This is equivalent to:

(Probability of 9 or more) + (Probability of 10 or more) + (Probability of 11 or more) + (Probability of 12 or more) + (Probability of 13 or more).

Given the demand distribution, the average number of stock-outs per lead time for any value of safety stock may be calculated.

The distribution of demand in the lead time is given in Table 5.2.

Table 5.2   Poisson distribution, mean = 6

Demand	Probability of this demand	Probability of this demand or more
0	0·00	1·00
1	0·02	1·00
2	0·04	0·98
3	0·09	0·94
4	0·14	0·85
5	0·16	0·71
6	0·16	0·55
7	0·14	0·39
8	0·10	0·25
9	0·07	0·15
10	0·04	0·08
11	0·02	0·04
12	0·01	0·02
13	0·01	0·01

Table 5.3 gives the average number of stock-outs per lead time for levels of safety stock from 0 to 7.

The expected stock-out cost per year is (average number of stock-outs per lead time) × (average number of replenishments per year) × (cost of a stock-out).

Table 5.3   Average number of stock-outs per lead time for various levels of safety stock

Safety stock	Average number of stock-outs per lead time
0	$0.39 + 0.25 + 0.15 + 0.08 + 0.04 + 0.02 + 0.01 = 0.94$
1	$0.25 + 0.15 + 0.08 + 0.04 + 0.02 + 0.01 = 0.55$
2	$0.15 + 0.08 + 0.04 + 0.02 + 0.01 = 0.30$
3	$0.08 + 0.04 + 0.02 + 0.01 = 0.15$
4	$0.04 + 0.02 + 0.01 = 0.07$
5	$0.02 + 0.01 = 0.03$
6	0.01
7	none

The average number of replenishments per year

$$= \frac{d}{Q} = \frac{300}{20} = 15$$

The cost of a stock-out is £40.

We are now in a position to compare the sums of the annual costs of stock-holding and stock-out for various levels of safety stock (see Table 5.4).

The entry in bold type in Table 5.4 indicates the lowest combined cost of stock-holding and stock-out. This corresponds to a safety stock of 4 items, which is the optimum level. Figure 5.6 shows in a histogram how the annual costs of stock-holding and stock-out depend on the level of safety stock.

In practice it is not necessary to enumerate all possibilities in order to determine the best level of safety stock. Just as it was possible to deduce mathematically a formula for the economic batch quantity, an expression relating the probability of a stock-out to the costs of stock-holding and stock-out can be derived. It can be shown that the optimum level of safety stock is the lowest which satisfies the following inequality:

Table 5.4 Comparison of the sums of the annual costs of stock-holding and stock-out for various levels of safety stock

Safety stock (a)	Stock-holding cost p.a. (b) = £30 × (a)	Average number of stock-outs per lead time (c) from Table 5.3	Expected stock-out cost p.a. (d) = £600 × (c)	Stock-holding plus stock-out cost p.a. (b) + (d)
0	0	0·94	£564	£564
1	£30	0·55	£330	£360
2	£60	0·30	£180	£240
3	£90	0·15	£90	£180
4	£120	0·07	£42	**£162**
5	£150	0·03	£18	£168
6	£180	0·01	£6	£186
7	£210	0	0	£210

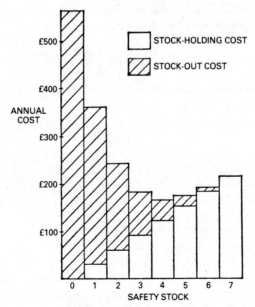

Fig. 5.6 Variation of stock-holding and stock-out cost with level of safety stock

The probability of stock-out $P_x \leqslant \dfrac{h}{h+s}$

where h = the cost of holding an extra item when it is not required – the *holding cost*

and s = the net cost of not holding an item when it is required – the *shortage cost*.

In the above example the cost of holding an item when it is not required is the cost of carrying an item from the receipt of one replenishment order to the receipt of the next, i.e. $\frac{1}{15}$ th of a year on average.

This cost is £ $\dfrac{ip}{15}$ or   £2

The net cost of not holding an item when it is required is *not* the same as the stock-out cost. Although the cost of a stock-out is incurred, one less item has to be carried in stock from the end of one lead time to the end of the next. The shortage cost is therefore £40 − £2, or £38. The optimum level of safety stock in the above example is the lowest which satisfies

$$P_x \leqslant \frac{0 \cdot 2}{0 \cdot 2 + 3 \cdot 8} \quad \text{or} \quad P_x \leqslant 0 \cdot 05$$

The probabilities of stock-out for various levels of safety stock are given in Table 5.5.

Table 5.5   Probabilities of stock-out for various levels of safety stock

Safety stock	Probability of stock-out
0	0·39
1	0·25
2	0·15
3	0·08
4	0·04
5	0·02
6	0·01
7	0

The lowest level of safety stock for which P_x is less than 0·05 is indicated in Table 5.5. This is 4 items, which confirms the value found by enumeration. The solution to Example 3 is that a replenishment order should be placed whenever the stock falls to 10 items. The size of the replenishment order should be 20 items.

Although the above analysis yields the optimum level of safety stock, it has limitations in situations where the cost of running out of stock cannot be readily found. In many situations it is by no means obvious what the true cost of late delivery, for example, is. It almost certainly depends on the customer concerned. In such cases it is useful to present graphically information on how much it costs the organisation, in terms of stock-holding, to provide given levels of customer service. For the item in Example 3, for instance, the average stock equals half the batch size plus the safety stock. The cost of holding half the batch size is

$$\frac{ipQ}{2}$$

i.e. £300 p.a. Table 5.6 compares, for various levels of safety stock, the annual cost of stock-holding with the number of stock-outs per year.

Table 5.6 Comparison of stock-holding cost with the number of stock-outs per year

Safety stock	Total annual stock-holding cost	Average number of stock-outs per year
0	£300	14·10
1	£330	8·25
2	£360	4·50
3	£390	2·25
4	£420	1·05
5	£450	0·45
6	£480	0·15
7	£510	none

If the warehouse stocks a thousand similar items, Fig. 5.7 shows graphically how much it costs the organisation to provide various levels of customer service.

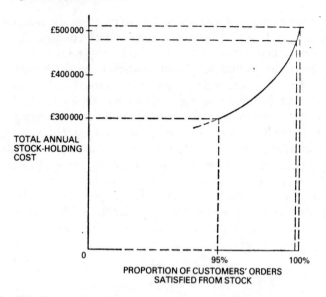

Fig. 5.7 Proportion of demand met from stock for different levels of stock investment

All but 5% of customers can be supplied from stock for an annual expenditure of £300 000. It costs an additional £210 000 however, to supply the final 5%, and £30 000 of this to supply the final 0·05%. Clearly, each increment of expenditure on stocks does not buy the same amount of customer satisfaction. When the cost of a stock-out is not measurable, Fig. 5.7 may well provide the basis for judging how much should be spent on stock-holding.

The periodic review system

The periodic review system is a convenient method of stock control when there are advantages to be gained from placing a batch of replenishment orders at the same time. It is also the most useful method of controlling the stocks of a company's finished products when, because of the nature of the production process, there is some preferred sequence of manufacture. A preferred sequence exists, for example, when, instead of there being a fixed set-up cost per batch, there is a cost in changing from one product to another which depends not only on the product to be made but also on the product being made previously. In this situation the products are most conveniently manufactured in production cycles and the problem becomes one of deciding how frequently a cycle should be started.

Derivation of the optimum frequency of production cycles
For any product in the production cycle,

let d = annual demand for the product
   r = production rate (in same units as d)
   q = quantity produced per cycle
   c = cost involved in changing over to this product from preceding product in the cycle
   p = production cost per item
   i = stock-holding cost p.a. (expressed as a fraction of stock value).
Also let n = the number of times the production cycle is carried out per year.

We note that three of the above variables are related by

$$q = \frac{d}{n} \qquad (1)$$

The average stock of any product equals half the maximum stock

$$= \frac{q}{2}\left(1 - \frac{d}{r}\right) \quad \text{(See page 76)}$$

Therefore the annual stock-holding cost

$$= \frac{ipq}{2}\left(1 - \frac{d}{r}\right)$$

which from (1) $= \frac{ipd}{2n}\left(1 - \frac{d}{r}\right)$

The annual change-over cost for any product $= nc$. Therefore the total variable costs for this product (stock-holding plus change-over)

$$= \frac{ipd}{2n}\left(1 - \frac{d}{r}\right) + nc$$

Similar expressions occur for all products made during the cycle and the total annual variable cost is the sum of all such expressions. Denoting the jth product in the cycle by the suffix j and using the summation sign Σ (sigma), the total annual variable cost

$$= \frac{i \Sigma p_j d_j \left(1 - \dfrac{d_j}{r_j}\right)}{2n} + n \Sigma c_j$$

Differentiating with respect to n

$$\frac{d}{dn} \text{ (annual variable cost)} = \frac{-i \Sigma p_j d_j \left(1 - \dfrac{d_j}{r_j}\right)}{2n^2} + \Sigma c_j$$

Equating to zero for a minimum value

$$\frac{i \Sigma p_j d_j \left(1 - \dfrac{d_j}{r_j}\right)}{2n^2} = \Sigma c_j$$

or

$$n = \sqrt{\frac{i \Sigma p_j d_j \left(1 - \dfrac{d_j}{r_j}\right)}{2 \Sigma c_j}}$$

The expression Σc_j is simply the sum of all change-over costs per cycle. If we call this c_{total} we obtain the following expression for the optimum number of production cycles per year:

$$n = \sqrt{\frac{i \Sigma p_j d_j \left(1 - \dfrac{d_j}{r_j}\right)}{2 c_{total}}}$$

The following example illustrates the use of the above formula.

EXAMPLE 4

A manufacturing company supplies from stock a group of five products. These are basically the same product produced in five different colours. All the products are manufactured on the same production unit of which the company has only one. Because of the nature of the product – it costs a small amount to change from a light colour to a darker one, but a much larger amount to make a change in the opposite direction – it is convenient to manufacture in a fixed sequence *ABCDE*. Using the notation above,

$$d_A = 2000 \text{ tons/year} \qquad c_{AB} = c_{BC} = c_{CD} = c_{DE} = £10$$
$$d_B = 1000 \text{ tons/year} \qquad c_{EA} = £260$$
$$d_C = 1000 \text{ tons/year} \qquad i = 0\cdot2 \text{ p.a.}$$
$$d_D = 250 \text{ tons/year} \qquad r = 5000 \text{ tons/year}$$
$$d_E = 250 \text{ tons/year}$$

The production cost is the same for all products and is £270 per ton. How frequently should the production cycle be repeated?

Solution   As *p* is the same for all products, the expression for the optimum frequency of production cycles reduces to

$$n = \sqrt{\frac{ip \, \Sigma \, d_j \left(1 - \dfrac{d_j}{r_j}\right)}{2c_{\text{total}}}}$$

Using the values above

$$n = \sqrt{\frac{0\cdot2 \times 270\left[2000\left(1 - \dfrac{2000}{5000}\right) + 2 \times 1000\left(1 - \dfrac{1000}{5000}\right) + 2 \times 250\left(1 - \dfrac{250}{5000}\right)\right]}{2(4 \times 10 + 260)}}$$

$$= \sqrt{\frac{0\cdot2 \times 270[1200 + 1600 + 475]}{2 \times 300}}$$

$$= \sqrt{294\cdot8} = 17\cdot2$$

The production cycle should be repeated 17·2 times a year, i.e. approximately every 3 weeks.

In order to take advantage of a production cycle from the point of view of stock control, it is essential that such a cycle operates regularly. Let us consider how the stock of product *A*, for example, can be effectively controlled.

EXAMPLE 5
The demand for product *A* is distributed Normally with a 4-weekly

mean of 180 tons and a standard deviation of 40 tons. The company's objective is to supply this product from stock, a stock-out occurring no more frequently than once a year. If the production department requires one week's notice of the exact amount to be made on each production run, derive a rule for deciding how much to make on each occasion.

Solution   The one week's notice required by the production department implies a lead time of one week between placing and starting to receive the replenishment order. The problem of when to place a replenishment order is, therefore, fixed as being one week before the production cycle starts.

Fig. 5.8 is a graphical representation of the periodic review system.

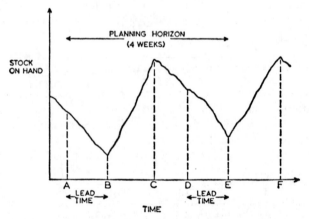

Fig. 5.8   Variation of stock level in a periodic review system

Points *A* and *D* (3 weeks apart) represent times when successive replenishment orders are placed on to the plant. Points *B* and *E* (also 3 weeks apart) show the times when these replenishment orders begin to be received into stock. Points *C* and *F* show the times when production of product *A* ceases. The problem is, how much should be ordered at point *A*?

After the replenishment order has been placed at point *A*, no further action can be taken until point *D*, and the results of this further action will not be felt until point *E*. This means that the time period which must be taken into account when replenishing the stock at point A is the 4-week period from A to E. The amount in stock at point A plus the amount ordered should be sufficient to meet the demands on the stock in this 4-week period.

There are approximately 17 replenishments per year. In order to have a stock-out only once a year on average, the probability of a stock-out per cycle must be $\frac{1}{17}$ or approximately 0·06. Because the demand is distributed Normally, we may obtain from a table of the Normal distribution that demand which is exceeded on only 6% of occasions. From Table 2.6 we see that this demand is the mean plus 1·55 standard deviations, i.e.

$$180 + 1\cdot55 \times 40 \quad \text{or} \quad 242 \text{ tons}.$$

The amount to order at point A is therefore 242 tons minus the amount in stock at this point. As a replenishment order is placed every 3 weeks, the average size of this order will be 3 weeks' demand or 135 tons.

Self-adaptive stock control

The reason why many stock control systems are inadequate is that they do not adapt to changing conditions. If a system is to keep abreast of changes in the patterns of demand or supply, it must include some method of forecasting.

The method of exponential smoothing described in Chapter 4 is particularly suitable for this purpose. To show how this may be used in stock control, consider the periodic review system of Example 5. The rule for stock replenishment was: order sufficient to bring the amount in stock plus that ordered to the mean demand in a 4-week period plus 1·55 standard deviations. Because the demand rate is unlikely to remain constant, a new forecast of this 4-weekly demand should be made every time a replenishment order is placed, according to the rule:

new forecast = old forecast + α(latest demand − old forecast)

and the rule for stock replenishment becomes:

order sufficient to bring the amount in stock plus that ordered to the latest forecast of the demand in a 4-week period plus 1·55 standard deviations.

In more sophisticated systems not only the demand forecast is updated each time the stock is reviewed, but also the standard deviation – which is now no longer the standard deviation of the 4-weekly demand but the standard deviation of the forecast error. Clearly, when one reaches this level of sophistication the amount of calculation may become considerable. These calculations are basically simple, however, and are ideally suited to a computer. If a computer is used to carry out all the calculations in connection with stock control, it may just as well store within it all the stock records, updating these daily using information of goods received and issued, and printing out daily the items to re-order.

Exercises

5.1 A product is sold at an average rate of 45 per day and can be manufactured at a rate of 450 per day. The set-up cost of the machine to produce the product is £10000 per batch and the stock-holding costs are 20% per annum of stock value. If labour charges are £4, materials £5 and overheads £6 per piece, determine the economic batch quantity and the total costs per piece. (Assume 300 days = 1 year.)

5.2 When a product is produced in economic batch quantities, the total variable costs (set-up + stock-holding) constitute 20% of the total costs per piece. What increase in the total cost per piece would ensue if the batch size was

(a) doubled?
(b) halved?

5.3 A contractor uses, from time to time, special pieces of earth-moving equipment. He may either obtain them on long-term hire for £10 per day and incur an additional cost of £20 per day to operate them when they are needed, or he can hire them on the day they are required for a cost of £50 per day (inclusive of operating cost). Past data indicate that the daily demand for the equipment follows a Poisson distribution with a mean of 2. How many pieces of equipment, if any, should the contractor obtain on long-term hire?

5.4 A company uses a raw material at an average rate of 30 tons per year. The cost incurred when a replenishment order is placed is £100 and the replenishment lead time is one month. The cost price per ton is £300 and the stock-holding cost is 20% per annum of stock value.

The company attempts to forecast its requirements for the material monthly and past records indicate that the distribution of forecast errors in this estimate has a mean of zero and a standard deviation of 500 kg. If the company's policy is not to run out of stock more frequently than once every five years, on average, how low should stock be allowed to fall before a replenishment is made, if the current monthly forecast is 2·75 tons? How much material should be ordered when a replenishment is necessary?

6

Queues

Introduction

There are many situations in daily life when a queue is formed if the service required by a customer is not immediately available. Due to the irregularity with which customers may arrive demanding service, and often also due to the variability in the time taken to satisfy different customers, queues may build up for a while. They may disappear during a lull in demand and then reappear.

The mathematical theory of queues consists of models of various types of such systems that enable one to predict how a system would cope, or fail to cope, with the demands put upon it. Consider the following five situations:

Situation 1

A post office offers a large variety of services to the public. Demand for these services varies through the day and during the week. The size of the waiting area is limited, so some customers may go away without being able to make any transaction. The time taken to complete a transaction (i.e. demand for a particular group of services) varies, due to counter layout and procedure and to the human capabilities involved.

Is it better for the public to have each kind of service available at different positions along the counter or to have all positions providing all services?

Situation 2
A telephone exchange has a certain number of operators. Subscribers may wish to make a call at any time, and in doing so they are quite unaware of others also wanting a number at the same time. If a subscriber does not get onto an operator immediately, he has to wait until one becomes free or else abandon his call. The time taken by the operator to complete the connection depends on the dialling requirements for the particular number and on how busy the system is. The time taken for the conversation itself is also variable.

How many operators should there be at different times of day to give reasonable service?

What does one mean by 'reasonable'?

Situation 3
A repairman looks after a number of different machines. Each machine may fail suddenly, producing no output until after the repairman has been able to repair and restart it. The chances of failure increase as the machines get older. The time taken to repair a machine varies.

What proportion of the time will the repairman not be occupied?

What is the chance of two or more machines being out of action simultaneously?

At what stage (if at all) is it worth hiring a second repairman to deal with the increasing number of failures?

Situation 4
An airport has one runway devoted to receiving landing aircraft. The precise times at which aircraft arrive from many directions cannot be controlled by the airport authority, even though the airlines have their schedules. Aircraft are delayed before takeoff, they may be helped by tail-winds or hindered by head-winds. On arrival over the airport an aircraft may be able to land immediately or may have to wait (be 'stacked'). There is a limit to the time which any aircraft can wait, related to the amount of fuel left in its tanks and the rate at which this is used up. When an aircraft lands, the time during which it occupies the runway and its approaches depends on the type of aircraft, the weather conditions, and the pilot.

What is the chance that an aircraft will have to wait before landing?

How high can this chance rise before the airport becomes effectively saturated?

How does this affect the airlines' plans for future flight schedules?

When a second runway is built, is it better to segregate types of aircraft into two groups, one for each runway, or not?

Situation 5

A stock of items in a warehouse is reduced from time to time when demands for that item occur. If there is a smaller number of items in stock than is demanded, the difference is often held-over until it can be met from a fresh supply of the item. Due to the variability in the occurrence of demands and the timing of replacement supplies, there are times when there are plenty of items in stock, as well as times when there are none and a back-log of demand.

What is the chance of being out-of-stock with a particular re-order system?

What is the cost of holding stock?

What is the cost of being out-of-stock?

How would you design a re-order system to minimise the average total cost of the system?

Variability of arrivals

In each of the situations described, an identifiable unit, whether a customer at a post office, a telephone caller, a machine failure, an aircraft, or a demand for stock, 'arrived' at some moment in time and required some form of 'service'. This chapter is concerned only with such discrete 'customers' arriving. Continuous variable arrivals, such as water in a reservoir waiting to be 'serviced' by electricity generators, are not considered.

It is often impossible to control the actual moment of arrival of a customer for service. Therefore the number of arrivals in one time period, or the length of time between successive arrivals, is not constant. A frequency distribution of either variable can be used to represent the variability of arrivals. Observations of an existing system have to be grouped into appropriately selected ranges from which a histogram is constructed. For theoretical analysis it is convenient to approximate the observed distribution by means of a theoretical probability distribution. Some important distributions were described in Chapter 2.

If the number of potential customers is infinitely large, then the probability of an arrival in the next time period does not depend on how many customers are already in the system. This assumption is frequently made and would probably be perfectly acceptable for four of the situations described. When, however, the number of potential customers is not only finite but also small, say 12, as might be the case in situation 3 with machine repairs, the probability of an arrival does depend on how many customers have already arrived. (In the extreme case with all 12 machines out of action, the probability of another machine failure is clearly zero.) Such a situation is said to involve 'cyclic' queues.

In a real system all customers may be alike, in terms of the variability of their arrivals and of the demands that they make on the service facility. Hence the situation involves only a single population. There may also be systems in which there are distinguishable groups of customers, for instance large and small aircraft. If the difference is significant, then the behaviour of the groups has to be described with separate frequency distributions.

The assumption in most queuing systems is that arrivals occur singly and hence two arrivals cannot occur simultaneously. Thus one is concerned only with the probability of 0 or 1 arrival in a small time period. There are, however, systems in which this is not a reasonable assumption. For example, bulk arrivals might necessarily be involved in the stock problem described in situation 5.

Service mechanism

The service mechanism at which customers arrive may be the most controllable feature of a queueing system. It may also involve a very large investment in physical facilities, so that proper analysis of the system and the best timing of an investment decision is important.

The simplest form of service mechanism is a single facility, through which all customers must pass if they are to be served. Once a customer has been through the service 'channel', he returns to the pool of potential customers for service again later on. More complicated systems arise when there are several channels, which may or may not have the same characteristics.

Multiple service channels may be arranged in parallel, so that a customer is served by any one channel. A single queue may form, from which a customer is drawn when the next channel becomes available; or a queue may form in front of each channel; or the number of queues may be greater than one but less than the number of channels. Banks, supermarkets and toll-booths are often arranged in this way.

Multiple service channels may also be arranged in series. Each customer may have to go through every channel or only through a specified selection of them. There may be only a single queue in front of the first channel, or it may be possible also to have intermediate queues between successive stages. Some manufacturing processes are of this kind.

It may be that there is a whole network of service channels, partly in parallel and partly in series. The flow of work through a jobbing machine shop might be arranged in this way.

The behaviour of queueing systems is affected not only by the number of channels involved and the way in which they are connected, but also by the reliability of the individual channels. This is seldom 100% (some warehouse shelving collapses, a telephone operator is taken ill, an airport runway is blocked by a crash), and leads to sudden additional pressure on other facilities. A system of service channels in parallel is obviously more robust to unreliability than a single channel or channels in series.

Queue discipline

The third feature of a queueing system is queue discipline, that is what actually happens between the moment of arrival of a customer wanting service and when service is actually being carried out.

The simplest discipline is for all arrivals to form a single queue and to wait until they receive service. In some situations there may be a fixed queue capacity, so that when the queue is at its maximum further customers arriving are turned away. Even without a limited queue capacity a customer may decide not to join the queue at all (balking), or he may join the queue but leave it again later if he has not started service before a certain time (reneging). In the case of multiple queues in parallel, it may be possible for a customer to change from the queue he first joined to another one, if he thinks that this would improve his chances of being through the system earlier (jockeying).

Given that there are certain customers arranged in some sort of queue at a moment in time, however they arrived there, there are different ways in which customers are transferred from the queue to the service channel when one becomes available. A classical discipline (FIFO = first in, first out) is for the customer who has been queueing the longest to be served next; thus the new arrival joins the back of the queue, waits until all those in front have been served, and then gets served himself. This is often considered to be 'fair' when customers are individual people. This could not be done, however, in telephone exchanges where the operator had no means of telling how long any caller had been trying to make the call, and therefore the callers were picked more or less at random. A third discipline for taking customers from the queue is the principle of LIFO = last, in first out. This may arise, for example, when 'customers' are sheets of paper piled on a warehouse floor; to remove the bottom sheet first would be difficult without inverting the whole pile, and to do so would merely repeat the dilemma the other way up.

It may also be possible to have a priority system of customer selection. Thus large and expensive aircraft might get priority in landing over smaller ones that had been waiting longer; large ships might get priority over small ships in entering a tidal lock because of the extra water needed. Priorities may be attached not to particular types of customers but to the state in which a customer arrives, e.g. patients requiring medical attention; or a combination of several factors.

None of the disciplines for transferring customers from the queue to the service channel necessarily affects the rate at which the channel operates; but the way in which waiting time is suffered by different customers is affected, and hence probably the overall economics of the system.

Variability of service times

Once a customer has started being served in a service channel, the time taken to complete the operation may be constant. More often, however, this time varies. It may be possible only to control the average characteristics of the service mechanism, not the performance achieved with a particular customer. Thus more and better training of operators may cut down the average service time, and perhaps also the variability of the service time; or investment in more expensive equipment may reduce the average time of an operation.

As in the case of measuring the variability of arrivals, the variability of service times can be measured by a frequency distribution. Observations of an existing system can be made and grouped into appropriately selected ranges from which a histogram is constructed.

It is often assumed that the service time and its variability is dependent only on the mechanism of the channel itself, and not on other variables such as the number of customers in the queue. However, in situations involving human customers, speed-up of this kind often occurs and tends to lead to constant queueing times regardless of how many customers are in the queue.

Service discipline

A service channel may handle only one customer at a time, e.g. a barber, but there can be systems in which customers are serviced in batches (bulk-service), e.g. bus-loads. In the latter case, customers in the queue may still wait when the service channel becomes free because there are not enough customers to be served together at that time.

Service may be operated on a basis of 'follow-on'. Once a customer (or batch) starts to be served, it continues until service is completed and then leaves this system. With certain types of priority systems, however, service can be 'pre-emptive'; a customer in service is disturbed by the arrival of a customer of higher priority, who gets put into service instead, and the service of the original, lower priority, customer is completed afterwards.

An approach to queueing theory

Having defined the operation of the particular system being studied, and measured the relevant variables and their frequency distributions, some sort of model is to be constructed. This must reproduce the effects of the present conditions of the system, as well as predict the effect of different conditions that might occur in the future. One line of attack to have been used in the analysis of queueing systems is to measure probabilities and then use probability theory to calculate variables of interest, such as the average time in the system (queueing and service). The advantage of this theoretical approach lies in the conciseness of results derived, so that substitution of the relevant values in a formula gives the required answer immediately. Its disadvantage arises because the calculation of such formulae is only possible when one is prepared to accept more or less restrictive assumptions about the system.

A simple queue

Consider a queueing system with the following properties:

    Discrete customers
    Infinite population of potential customers
    Variable arrivals
    No simultaneous arrivals
    Single service channel
    Single queue, infinite capacity
    First come, first served queue discipline
    Single, follow-on service discipline
    Variable service times

When the variability of the number of customers arriving in a given interval (1 minute, 1 hour, etc.), and of the number of customers having completed service in that interval, can be described by a Poisson distribution (see Chapter 2), then the resulting system is often called a 'simple queue'. Assuming that the system has been in operation long enough for it to have settled down, some simple results about average characteristics (such as time in the system) have been derived. The analysis of the dynamics of queues, for example just after the system has started operating, is more difficult and results for this situation are not quoted here.

An important measure of a simple queue is its traffic intensity, where

$$\text{traffic intensity} = \frac{\text{mean rate of arrival}}{\text{mean rate of service}}$$

or
$$\varrho = \frac{\lambda}{\mu}$$

(It is conventional in queueing theory to use the Greek symbols, ϱ (rho)*, λ (lambda) and μ (mu), for these variables.)

It is a peculiarity of this system that:

$$\text{mean inter-arrival time} = \frac{1}{\text{mean rate of arrival}}$$

and

$$\text{mean service time} = \frac{1}{\text{mean rate of service}}$$

so that an alternative equation for ϱ is:

$$\text{traffic intensity} = \frac{\text{mean service time}}{\text{mean inter-arrival time}}$$

or

$$\varrho = \frac{1/\mu}{1/\lambda}$$

A necessary condition for the system to have settled down is that the traffic intensity is less than 1, i.e. that the average rate of arrival is less than the average rate of service. If this is not so, the size of the queue tends to get larger and larger as time goes on (remember that we have assumed that the rate of service is not affected by the length of queue). If there is no traffic, then clearly the traffic intensity is 0. It is because so many aspects of queueing systems are not directly proportional to the traffic intensity that the mathematical analysis of queues becomes worth doing.

Some results
It can be shown (see bibliography) that, for a simple queue and a traffic intensity less than 1:

Probability of a customer having to wait for service $= \varrho$

Average number of customers in the system $= \dfrac{\varrho}{1 - \varrho}$

---

* Also to be found printed as the symbol ρ.

Average number of customers in the queue (including occasions when the queue length is zero)

$$= \frac{\varrho^2}{1 - \varrho}$$

Average number of customers in the queue when there is a queue

$$= \frac{1}{1 - \varrho}$$

Average time a customer is in the system

$$= \frac{1}{1 - \varrho} \times \frac{1}{\mu}$$

Average time a customer is in the queue

$$= \frac{\varrho}{1 - \varrho} \times \frac{1}{\mu}$$

Thus, if the values of μ and ϱ are known, it is easy to deduce, by using these formulae, something about the simple queue system. All except the last two equations do not depend on the units of μ; ϱ is a ratio.

EXAMPLE 1

For a simple queue, what is the average number of customers in the system for a traffic intensity of 0·5, 0·8, 0·9 and 0·95?

Solution

ϱ	$1 - \varrho$	$\varrho/1 - \varrho$	= average number
0·5	0·5	1	of customers in
0·8	0·2	4	the system
0·9	0·1	9	
0·95	0·05	19	

EXAMPLE 2

If the mean service rate is 10 per hour, what is the average time a customer is in the queue for the same traffic intensities?

Solution

ϱ	$\dfrac{\varrho}{1 - \varrho}$	$\dfrac{\varrho}{1 - \varrho} \times \dfrac{1}{\mu} =$	average time a customer is in
0·5	1	0·1 hours	the queue
0·8	4	0·4	
0·9	9	0·9	
0·95	19	1·9	

Thus when the traffic intensity is as high as 0·95, customers will have to wait in the queue for 114 minutes (on average) before being served in 6 minutes (on average).

Some further results: channels in parallel

Suppose that there are a number, say c, of identical service channels arranged in parallel. The customer at the front of a single queue is served by whichever channel becomes available next. If the system is identical in all other respects with the simple queue, whose properties were specified above, how different are the results?

The traffic intensity of the system becomes:

$$= \frac{\text{mean rate of arrival}}{c \times \text{mean rate of service of a single channel}}$$

or $\varrho = \dfrac{\lambda}{c\mu}$

or $\varrho = \dfrac{1/\mu}{c/\lambda}$

As before, a necessary condition for the system to settle down is that the traffic intensity must be less than 1, i.e.

$$\frac{\lambda}{c\mu} < 1$$

or $$\lambda < c\mu$$

Given that this is so, the results for the average number of customers in the system, etc., are more complicated than for the single channel case, since the number of channels, c, is also involved. It is convenient to write the results in terms of c, the traffic intensity ϱ, the probability that there are no customers in the system P_0, and the mean service rate at each channel, μ.

Probability of a customer having to wait for service $= \dfrac{(\varrho c)^c}{c!(1 - \varrho)} P_0$

Average number of customers in the system $= \dfrac{\varrho(\varrho c)^c}{c!(1 - \varrho)^2} P_0 + \varrho c$

Average number of customers in the queue $= \dfrac{\varrho(\varrho c)^c}{c!(1 - \varrho)^2} P_0$

Average time a customer is in the system $= \dfrac{(\varrho c)^c}{c!(1 - \varrho)^2 c\mu} P_0 + \dfrac{1}{\mu}$

Average time a customer is in the queue $= \dfrac{(\varrho c)^c}{c!(1-\varrho)^2 c\mu} P_0$

The probability that there are no customers in any of the service channels, P_0, is related to the number of channels, c, and the traffic intensity, ϱ, by the equation:

$$P_0 = \frac{c!(1-\varrho)}{(\varrho c)^c + c!(1-\varrho)\left\{\displaystyle\sum_{n=0}^{c-1} \frac{1}{n!}(\varrho c)^n\right\}}$$

EXAMPLE 3

Find the probability that there are no customers in the system, given that:

(i) number of channels in parallel = 3
(ii) mean arrival rate = 24 per hour
(iii) mean service rate of each channel = 10 per hour

Solution The traffic intensity, $\varrho = \dfrac{\lambda}{c\mu} = \dfrac{24}{3 \times 10} = 0.8$.

The number of channels, $c = 3$.

Hence, substituting these values into the equation for P_0,

$$P_0 = \frac{3 \times 2 \times 1 \times (1-0.8)}{(0.8 \times 3)^3 + 3 \times 2 \times 1 \times (1-0.8)\{1 + (0.8 \times 3) + (0.8 \times 3)^2/2\}}$$

$$= \frac{6(0.2)}{(2.4)^3 + 6(0.2)(1 + 2.4 + (2.4)^2/2)}$$

$$= \frac{1.2}{13.82 + 1.2(6.3)}$$

$$= 0.056$$

Thus, with a traffic intensity of 0.8, the system will be completely idle for about 6% of the time.

EXAMPLE 4

Given that the mean arrival rate is 24 per hour as before, compare the average time a customer is in the system for the following two systems:

(a) 3 channels in parallel, each with a mean service rate of 10 per hour.

(b) 1 channel with a mean service rate of 30 per hour.

Solution

(a) In Example 3, it was shown that for $c = 3$,

$$\mu = 10$$

then $\varrho = 0.8$ and $P_0 = 0.056$

Therefore, for channels in parallel the average time a customer is in the system

$$= \frac{(\varrho c)^c}{c!(1 - \varrho)^2 c\mu} P_0 + \frac{1}{\mu}$$

$$= \frac{(0.8 \times 3)^3}{3 \times 2 \times 1 \times (1 - 0.8)^2 3 \times 10} 0.056 + \frac{1}{10}$$

$$= \frac{(2.4)^3 0.056}{6(0.2)^2 30} + 0.1$$

$$= 0.11 + 0.10$$

$$= 0.21 \text{ hours} = 12.6 \text{ minutes}$$

(b) For a single channel and $\mu = 30$,

then $$\varrho = \frac{24}{30} = 0.8$$

the same traffic intensity as for (a).

But in this case, being a single channel, the average time a customer is in the system

$$= \frac{1}{1 - \varrho} \times \frac{1}{\mu}$$

$$= \frac{1}{1 - 0.8} \times \frac{1}{30}$$

$$= \frac{1}{0.2 \times 30}$$

$$= \tfrac{1}{6} \text{ hours} = 10 \text{ minutes}$$

Since both (*a*) and (*b*) involve the same traffic intensity, it is clear that customers receive better service from a single faster channel than from several slower channels in parallel. If the cost of the single fast channel is no more than the total cost of the slower channels, then it is not worth having more than one channel anyway. If the cost of the single fast channel is greater than the total cost of the slower channels, then it will still be worth having the single channel, provided that the value of the time saved is more than the extra cost of the single fast channel. This reasoning assumes that the service channels do not break down. But if this is likely to occur, one would want to compare the relative values of:

(i) a more expensive and reliable channel
(ii) several independent channels to spread risk of breakdowns
(iii) different customer service achieved with alternative systems.

Such a comparison would include some of the considerations raised in this chapter.

Channels in series

When the output of one service channel is the input to another, further questions arise. For instance, should the service rate of each successive channel be the same, or increasing? Is the variability in the rate at which customers arrive at the first channel the same as the variability of arrivals at the second channel? If not, is the latter greater than the former, or less?

For the simple queue described earlier and with a traffic intensity of less than 1, it turns out that the variability of arrivals at each successive channel is the same. Therefore provided that there is some excess capacity, the service rate at each channel can be the same. The series of channels may then be regarded as 'balanced' though deliberately under-utilised. For other systems, when arrivals get more and more variable at each successive channel, not only must there be spare capacity but also increasing service rates at the later stages to deal adequately with the increased variability. In this case, the line is again deliberately under-utilised (i.e. traffic intensity less than 1) but now with 'unbalanced' service rates.

The analysis of such systems, especially when there may be channels in series and in parallel involved, is beyond the scope of this text but is an interesting area for exploration, especially by simulation.

Monte Carlo simulation – a queueing application

The queueing theory results quoted in the preceding section are, of course, only a small fraction of those that have been derived. The mathematical analysis involved requires expert knowledge and is not pursued here. Enough of the general approach, and of the kind of answers that are obtainable, has been given to indicate the nature of queueing theory. But what happens when the system of interest is such that it cannot be represented adequately by any of the theoretical models for which results have been calculated? Here a quite different approach can be adopted, namely simulation.

Simulation is simply a means of creating a typical life-history of the system under given conditions, working out step-by-step what happens to each customer as he arrives and passes through the different parts of the system. In order to do this, one needs to know the detailed characteristics and rules of operation of the system, and to have the relevant measures of the system. The effect of variability on the system as a whole is reproduced by sampling from the relevant distributions. For example, sampling from a distribution of the time interval between successive arrivals produces a typical sequence of moments when a customer arrives. Similarly, sampling from a service time distribution gives a typical sequence of the time taken by each customer to be served. The interaction between these can be worked out and hence the time of arrival and departure is determined for each customer. From this sample the average time in the system, for example, is calculated. When the simulation is carried out for existing conditions, a check is made to see that the correspondence between actual results and the simulation results is sufficiently close. Then the simulation can be used again, for different conditions that might arise in the future, in order to predict the likely effects of new conditions. Thus it is possible to experiment with the simulation in a very direct way that is impossible with the system itself.

The procedure of sampling from a distribution is similar to spinning a roulette wheel in order to determine the next value.

However it is inconvenient to do the sampling in t
practice it is easier either to use random numbers, or fo
systems to use special computer-simulation programs whic
automatic procedures for sampling from any specified disti
The effort involved in simulation is such that little developi ~nt of
the technique would have occurred without the use of computers.
Even with a computer it is desirable to build as many short cuts as
possible into the simulation, provided that they do not lead to
unacceptable loss of accuracy. Simulation of systems has been
carried out in many contexts, such as with various production
scheduling and stock control systems. But it will be illustrated here
with an example of a hypothetical airport.

EXAMPLE 5

An airport with two runways receives a succession of large and small
aircraft in equal proportions and at irregular intervals. The time that
a runway is effectively occupied by an aircraft during its approach
and landing is variable, and it is longer on the average for large
aircraft.

At present one runway receives the small aircraft and the other
the large aircraft. The airport authority is considering making both
runways capable of taking either type of aircraft. To justify the
investment involved a substantially better service would have to be
available by doing so.

Compare the present system and the proposed future system,
given the following data on the irregularity of arrivals and the
service times for large and small aircraft.

Data

1 *Inter-arrival time distribution*

Range, min	Mid pt of range	%	Cumulative %
0–2	1	9	9
2–4	3	18	27
4–6	5	26	53
6–8	7	20	73
8–10	9	15	88
10–12	11	12	100

Average: 6·00 minutes

2   *Type of aircraft distribution*

	%
Large	50
Small	50

3   *Service time distribution (large aircraft)*

Range, min	Mid pt of range	%	Cumulative %
0–2	1	0	0
2–4	3	0	0
4–6	5	0	0
6–8	7	0	0
8–10	9	22	22
10–12	11	41	63
12–14	13	28	91
14–16	15	9	100

Average: 11·48 minutes

4   *Service time distribution (small aircraft)*

Range, min	Mid pt of range	%	Cumulative %
0–2	1	0	0
2–4	3	0	0
4–6	5	16	16
6–8	7	27	43
8–10	9	39	82
10–12	11	18	100
12–14	13	0	100
14–16	15	0	100

Average: 8·18 minutes

Solution

1   *Arrivals*   Since the inter-arrival time distributions of the two types of aircraft have been found to be indistinguishable and represented by the single distribution, data 1, the succession of arrivals is found by sampling from this distribution. Then at each moment of time when an arrival occurs, sampling from the distribution, data 2, determines the type of aircraft of this particular arrival. In this case a penny could be tossed as the two percentages are equal.

Table 6.1 Typical succession of the first 30 arrivals

2-digit random numbers	Inter-arrival time, min	Type of aircraft	Clock time of arrivals, min	
			Large	Small
19	3	L	03	
01	1	S		04
65	7	S		11
62	7	S		18
39	5	L	23	
85	9	L	32	
48	5	S		37
83	9	L	46	
10	3	S		49
39	5	L	54	
14	3	S		57
90	11	L	68	
44	5	L	73	
67	7	L	80	
92	11	S		91
02	1	L	92	
39	5	L	97	
57	7	S		104
01	1	S		105
63	7	L	112	
79	9	S		121
23	3	L	124	
81	9	S		133
88	11	L	144	
50	5	S		149
29	5	S		154
90	11	S		165
75	9	L	174	
34	5	S		179
58	7	S		186

Thus the first 30 arrivals might follow a pattern such as given in Table 6.1. The derivation of this table is given immediately below.

Column 1 is a sequence of 2-digit random numbers. These may be thought of as the result of spinning a roulette wheel, marked with 100 divisions, labelled 00 to 99. Each number is equally likely and will appear at random. Then these are used to derive inter-arrival times having the required distribution by the allocation.

Random number	Inter-arrival time, min
00–08	1
09–26	3
27–52	5
53–72	7
73–87	9
88–99	11

Thus the first random number, 19, falls in the range 09 to 26, so the first inter-arrival time is 3 minutes. The second random number, 01, is in the range 00 to 08, so the second inter-arrival time is 1 minute; and so on throughout the sequence. As the length of the sequence increases the distribution of the inter-arrival times sampled approaches more and more closely the original generating distribution, data 1. For the 30 numbers sampled in this example the fit is reasonably close, but in general a sample of many more than 30 would be needed to ensure this.

Inter-arrival time, min	Sample of 30		Original data 1
	Frequency	%	%
1	3	10	9
3	4	13	18
5	8	27	26
7	6	20	20
9	5	17	15
11	4	13	12
	—	—	—
	30	100	100
	—	—	—

Column 3 is the sequence of large and small aircraft, determined by the oddness or evenness of a series of 1-digit random numbers (equivalent to tossing a penny). In this case there are 14 large aircraft and 16 small aircraft in the first 30 arrivals.

Knowing the type of aircraft and the inter-arrival times, the clock-time at which each aircraft arrives is immediately determined by progressively adding up the inter-arrival times. For convenience the results have been sorted into those for large aircraft (col. 4) and those for small aircraft (col. 5).

2 *Service times (large aircraft)* In order to calculate typical service times for the 14 large aircraft in the sample of 30, more 2-digit random numbers are required, and the service time is determined by the allocation:

Random number	Service time, min
00–21	9
22–62	11
63–90	13
91–99	15

This allocation will give service times having the required distribution, data 3.

2-digit random numbers	Service time, min
82	13
45	11
60	11
19	9
23	11
77	13
31	11
96	15
04	9
68	13
90	13
11	9
57	11
42	11

The first random number, 82, falls in the range 63 to 90, so the first service time is 13 minutes; and so on. In this small sample of 14, the comparison between the service times sampled and the original distribution is:

Service time, min	Sample of 14		Original data 3
	Frequency	%	%
9	3	21	22
11	6	43	41
13	4	29	28
15	1	7	9
	——	——	——
	14	100	100
	——	——	——

3 *Service times (small aircraft)* In order to calculate typical service times for the 16 small aircraft in the sample of 30, further 2-digit random numbers are used, and the service time is determined by the allocation:

Random number	Service time, min
00–15	5
16–42	7
43–81	9
82–99	11

This allocation will give service times having the required distribution, data 4.

2-digit random numbers	Service time, min
55	9
85	11
63	9
42	7
00	5
79	9
91	11
22	7
49	9
01	5
41	7
99	11
51	9
40	7
36	7
65	9

The first random number falls in the range 43 to 81, so the first service time is 9 minutes; and so on. In this sample of 16, the comparison between the service times sampled and the original distribution is:

Service time, min	Sample of 16 Frequency	%	Original data 4 %
5	2	12	16
7	5	31	27
9	6	38	39
11	3	19	18
	16	100	100

4 *Simulation* Having determined the arrival times and service times with the required variabilities of the first 30 aircraft, we can compare the present system, *A* (of separate runways for the two types of aircraft), and the proposed system, *B* (both runways taking any aircraft).

Table 6.2 System A, *first* runway, large aircraft

Present system A

Arrival no. (1)	Clock time of arrival (2)	Clock time of start of service (3)	Service time (4)	Clock time of end of service (5)	Waiting time (runway) (6)	Waiting time (aircraft-minutes) (7)
1	03	03	13	16	3	
2	23	23	11	34	7	
3	32	34	11	45		2
4	46	46	9	55	1	
5	54	55	11	66		1
6	68	68	13	81	2	
7	73	81	11	92		8
8	80	92	15	107		12
9	92	107	9	116		15
10	97	116	13	129		19
11	112	129	13	142		17
12	124	142	9	151		18
13	144	151	11	162		7
14	174	174	11	185	12	
			160		25	99

Column 2 is column 4 in Table 6.1, Arrivals.

Column 4 is the service times determined in para. 2.

The figure in column 3 is the same as in column 2 if the runway is free when the aircraft arrives; and it is the same as in column 5 for the previous aircraft if the runway is in use when the aircraft arrives.

Column 5 is the sum of column 3 and column 4.

Column 6 is the difference between the end of service of one aircraft and the beginning of service of the next (when this is positive), i.e. when the runway is idle.

Column 7 is the difference between column 2 and column 3 when this is positive, i.e. when the aircraft has to wait.

The first runway is, in this sample, in the various states for the following times:

No aircraft in the system	25 minutes
1 aircraft but no queue	81
A queue with 1 aircraft	59
A queue with 2 aircraft	20
A queue with more than 2 aircraft	0
	185 minutes

The total time during which the aircraft were actually using the first runway was 160 minutes (= 185 − 25).

The calculations in Table 6.3 are exactly the same as in the previous table but using the relevant data for small rather than large aircraft.

The second runway is, in the sample, in the various states for the following times:

No aircraft in the system	63 minutes
1 aircraft but no queue	108
A queue with 1 aircraft	24
A queue with more than 1 aircraft	0
	195 minutes

Table 6.3 System A, *second* runway, small aircraft

Arrival no. (1)	Clock time of arrival (2)	Clock time of start of service (3)	Service time (4)	Clock time of end of service (5)	Waiting time (runway) (6)	Waiting time (aircraft-minutes) (7)
1	04	04	9	13	4	
2	11	13	11	24		2
3	18	24	9	33		6
4	37	37	7	44	4	
5	49	49	5	54	5	
6	57	57	9	66	3	
7	91	91	11	102	25	
8	104	104	7	111	2	
9	105	111	9	120		6
10	121	121	5	126	1	
11	133	133	7	140	7	
12	149	149	11	160	9	
13	154	160	9	169		6
14	165	169	7	176		4
15	179	179	7	186	3	
16	186	186	9	195		
			132		63	24

The total time during which the aircraft were using the second runway was 132 minutes ($= 195 - 63$).

Proposed system B. System B is a single system of two channels in parallel, with a single queue, first-come-first-served. The service time of each channel depends on the type of aircraft. Assuming that an aircraft goes to the first runway if both are free, but to the vacant one if only one is free, and using exactly the same pattern of arrivals and variability of service times, the simulation of the first 30 arrivals is shown in Table 6.4.

Table 6.4 System B, both runways, large and small aircraft

| Clock time of arrivals min | | First runway | | | Second runway | | | Waiting time | | Waiting time | |
Large (1)	Small (2)	Start of service (3)	Service time (4)	End of service (5)	Start of service (6)	Service time (7)	End of service (8)	First runway (9)	Second runway (10)	Large aircraft, min (11)	Small aircraft, min (12)
03		03	13	16				3			
	04				04	9	13		4		2
	11				13	11	24				
	18	18	9	27				2			
23					24	11	35			1	
32		32	11	43				5			
	37				37	7	44		2		
46		46	9	55				3			
	49				49	5	54		5		
54					54	11	65				
	57	57	9	66				2			
68		68	13	81				2			
73					73	11	84		8		
80		81	15	96						1	

									30	68	16	11
92	91	96	9	105	91	11	102			7	4	1
97	104	105	7	112	102	13	115	9			5	7
	105	112	9	121								
112	121	121	5	126	115	13	128				3	
		126	9	135				1		5		
124	133	144	11	155	133	7	140	2	9	9	2	
144	149	155	9	164	149	11	160					
	154	165	7	172				1		19		1
	165	174	11	185								
174	179	186	9	195	179	7	186			9		
	186				195							
			165			127		30	68	16	11	

Column 1 is column 2 in Table 6.2.
Column 2 is column 2 in Table 6.3.
Column 3 is:

(i) *If there is no queue*
the time of arrival of the next aircraft allocated to first runway; therefore column 3 = column 1 (large aircraft) or column 3 = column 2 (small aircraft).

(ii) *If there is a queue*
the time of end of service of the previous aircraft on the first runway; therefore time in column 3 for this aircraft = time in column 5 for previous aircraft.

Columns 4 and 7 are service times, sampled from the relevant distributions for large and small aircraft. Since both runways are being used by both types of aircraft, columns 4 and 7 taken together are the combination of column 4 in Table 6.2 and column 4 in Table 6.3.

Column 5 = column 3 + column 4.
Column 6 is:

(i) *If there is no queue*
the time of arrival of the next aircraft allocated to the second runway; therefore column 6 = column 1 (large aircraft) or column 6 = column 2 (small aircraft).

(ii) *If there is a queue*
the time of end of service of the previous aircraft on the second runway; therefore time in column 6 for this aircraft = time in column 8 for previous aircraft.

Column 7: see column 4.
Column 8 = column 6 + column 7.
Column 9 is the difference (when it is positive) between the end of service of one aircraft and the beginning of service of the next aircraft on the first runway, i.e. when the runway is idle.
Column 10 is as for column 9 but for the second runway.
Column 11 is the difference (when it is positive) between the arrival time of large aircraft and the start of service for that aircraft, i.e. when a large aircraft waits.
Column 12 is as for column 11 but for small aircraft.

The reader is encouraged to work through Table 6.4 row-by-row to see how each aircraft is handled in this simulation.

Comparison of system A and system B. The waiting time of aircraft of both kinds is larger with system *A* than it is with the more flexible system *B*. This is measured by the total of column 7 in Table 6.2, column 7 in Table 6.3, and columns 11 and 12 in Table 6.4.

	Waiting time, aircraft-minutes	
	system A	*system B*
Large aircraft	99	16
Small aircraft	24	11

Whether such results are reliable depends on the size of the sample simulated. In this case 30 arrivals is definitely not adequate, but no doubt the reader is glad to be spared a larger sample on this occasion.

Whether system *B* is economically justifiable depends on the cost of the system and on the value of aircraft waiting time, as well as many other factors concerning airports that have been ignored for the purposes of this example.

Other applications of simulation techniques

In this chapter the focus has been on queues, and an indication has been given of the Monte Carlo simulation technique for studying their behaviour. The usefulness of this technique is not confined to congestion problems; other successful applications have been achieved. Also, forms of simulation techniques not of the Monte Carlo variety have been developed, and may be more appropriate in a particular situation.

Exercises

6.1 (*a*) What is the condition for a 'simple queue' system to be statistically stable?

(*b*) What tends to happen if this condition does not hold?

6.2 How does the average time a customer is in a simple queue system vary with the traffic intensity, if the average service rate is 10 per hour?

6.3 Given an average arrival rate of 22 per hour, is it better for the customer to get service at a single channel (mean service rate = 23 per hour) or at one of two channels in parallel (mean service rate = 12 per hour in both channels)?

6.4 Plot on a time scale the simulations given in Tables 6.2, 6.3 and 6.4.

7

Linear Programming

Introduction

The problem of how to utilise limited resources to the best advantage is a familiar one. Mathematical programming is the name given to a set of techniques developed to tackle this type of problem. Linear programming, the simplest and most widely used of these techniques, is a method for deciding how to meet some desired objective, such as minimising cost or maximising profit, subject to constraints on the amounts of commodities required or resources available.

The term linearity implies proportionality. This simply means that if 1 kg of a commodity costs £1, 10 kg will cost £10; if a steel rolling mill can produce 200 tons in 1 hour, it can produce 1000 tons in 5 hours.

Sometimes there are economies to be derived from increasing the scale of an operation such that the assumption of linearity does not hold. However, within limits this proportionality usually exists, at least approximately, and hence the principles of linear programming have been found to be of wide application. An example will best illustrate the type of problem to which linear programming is relevant.

EXAMPLE 1

A manufacturer makes two types of product, I and II. Three machines A, B, and C are required for the manufacture of each product. One unit of product I requires 2 hours on machine A, 1 on machine B and 6 on machine C, whilst one unit of product II requires, respectively, 2 hours, 5 hours and 2 hours on machines A, B, and C. In a given period there are 24 hours available on machine A, 44 on machine B and 60 on machine C. The profit per unit on product I is £6 and on product II is £9. Given that machines are available when required, how many units of each product should be made in order to maximise profit?

Formulation of problem   Let x_1 be the number of units of product I produced and x_2 be the number of units of product II produced.

Each of the x_1 units of product I and the x_2 units of product II requires 2 hours on machine A, i.e. a total of $2x_1 + 2x_2$ hours is required. The restriction on there being only 24 hours available on this machine means that $2x_1 + 2x_2$ must be less than or equal to 24. This may be represented algebraically by the inequality

$$2x_1 + 2x_2 \leqslant 24$$

Similarly, the constraints imposed by machines B and C may be represented by $x_1 + 5x_2 \leqslant 44$ and $6x_1 + 2x_2 \leqslant 60$ respectively. The objective is to maximise profit which is represented by the function $6x_1 + 9x_2$. Finally, neither x_1 nor x_2 can be negative (it is impossible to produce less than nothing of either product), and so the problem can be stated in mathematical terms as follows:

Maximise	$6x_1 + 9x_2$	(objective function)	(1)
subject to	$\left.\begin{array}{l} x_1 \geqslant 0 \\ x_2 \geqslant 0 \end{array}\right\}$	—	(2)
and	$\left.\begin{array}{l} 2x_1 + 2x_2 \leqslant 24 \\ x_1 + 5x_2 \leqslant 44 \\ 6x_1 + 2x_2 \leqslant 60 \end{array}\right\}$	—	(3)

This is the standard formulation of a linear programming problem. Any pair of values of x_1 and x_2 which satisfies the sets of inequalities (2) and (3) is a *feasible* solution to the problem. An *optimal* solution is a feasible solution which also satisfies (1).

Solution   As the problem consists of only two variables, x_1 and x_2, we may use a graphical method to obtain the solution. An equation of the form $2x_1 + 2x_2 = 24$ defines a straight line in the x_1, x_2 plane (see Figure 7.1). An inequality, therefore, defines an area bounded by a straight line. Region A (Figure 7.1), up to and including the

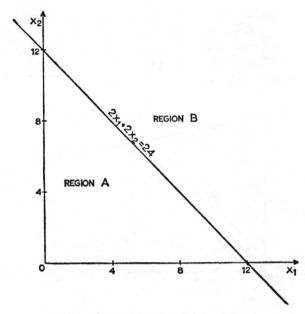

Fig. 7.1 Graph of $2x_1 + 2x_2 = 24$

straight line, is defined by $2x_1 + 2x_2 \leqslant 24$, whilst region *B* is defined by $2x_1 + 2x_2 \geqslant 24$. We may, by construction, obtain that region which satisfies the sets of inequalities (2) and (3). This is illustrated in Fig. 7.2.

The region shaded contains all pairs of values of x_1 and x_2 which are feasible solutions to the problem: hence its name – the *feasible region*. Within this region we seek to maximise the objective function (profit) $6x_1 + 9x_2$.

There are various pairs of values of x_1 and x_2 which lead to the same profit. A profit of £36, for instance, would be obtained for all pairs of values of x_1 and x_2 satisfying the equation $6x_1 + 9x_2 = 36$, i.e. lying on the objective function line drawn in Fig. 7.3. The objective function line for any other profit would be a line parallel to the one drawn. This line would be nearer to the origin for a smaller profit, but would become further removed from the origin as the profit increased. The maximum value of the objective function which satisfies all the constraints is determined by finding that point

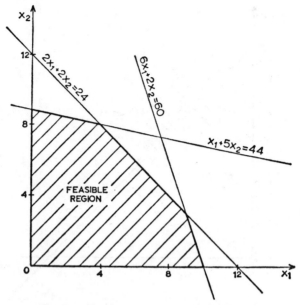

Fig. 7.2 The feasible region of Example 1

which, although within the feasible region, lies on a line parallel to the objective function line of Fig. 7.3, as far removed as possible from the origin. It can be seen from Fig. 7.3 that point Q is such a point.

The values of x_1 and x_2 corresponding to point Q may be read from the graph. They are $x_1 = 4$, $x_2 = 8$. Maximum profit is obtained by producing 4 units of product I and 8 units of product II and this profit is $(4 \times £6) + (8 \times £9)$ or £96.

Substituting the values of x_1 and x_2 in the set of inequalities (3), we see that the first two inequalities are satisfied as equations. This means that machines A and B are fully utilised. There is, however, spare capacity of 20 hours on machine C. The fact that machines A and B are fully utilised can be deduced directly from the graph by noting that point Q lies at the intersection of the lines $2x_1 + 2x_2 = 24$ and $x_1 + 5x_2 = 44$.

In any linear programming problem consisting of two variables, the feasible region may be represented graphically, as in the above

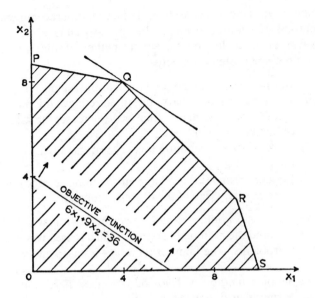

Fig. 7.3 Graphical solution of Example 1

example, by a convex polygon, i.e. a straight-edged figure with all internal angles less than 180°. It may also be noted, by reference to Fig. 7.3, that a linear objective function must attain its maximum value at a vertex or *extreme point* of such a region. If the objective function happens to be parallel to one of the edges of the feasible region, then any point along this edge – which includes the extreme points at both ends – maximises the objective function. When this is so, the optimal solution is not unique; indeed, there is an infinite number of optimal solutions.

The graphical method of solution may be extended to the case where there are three products, i.e. three variables x_1, x_2 and x_3. In this case each constraint is represented by a plane in the three dimensions x_1, x_2 and x_3, and the feasible region bounded by these planes is a convex polyhedron. As in the two-variable case, the objective function attains its maximum value at an extreme point of the three dimensional feasible region.

The graphical method is obviously of no practical value when the number of variables exceeds three. In fact, it is not recommended as a method of solution even in the three-variable case. It does, however, afford a clue to a systematic method of solution of linear programming problems, namely:

(i) Locate an extreme point of the feasible region.
(ii) Examine each boundary edge intersecting at this point to see whether movement along any edge increases the value of the objective function.
(iii) If this is so, move along this edge to the adjacent extreme point.
(iv) Repeat (ii) and (iii) until movement along an edge no longer increases the value of the objective function.

This approach would certainly give the optimum solution in Example 1, and the method of solution which is used to solve more complex problems – the Simplex method – is based on this reasoning.

The Simplex method will not be described here, but consists purely of simple arithmetic steps, and is ideally suited for solution using a computer. Standard linear programming computer prorams have been prepared for most computers such that the only preparation necessary is for the data to be fed into the computer in some predetermined manner. The results of a calculation which may have taken several days to perform manually may be obtained from a computer in a matter of seconds.

Statement of the general linear programming problem

Having considered and solved a simple example we now formulate the general linear programming problem, namely:

Maximise
$$c_1x_1 + c_2x_2 + \ldots + c_nx_n \qquad \text{(objective function)} \qquad (4)$$

subject to
$$\left. \begin{array}{l} x_1 \geqslant 0 \\ x_2 \geqslant 0 \\ \cdot \\ \cdot \\ \cdot \\ x_n \geqslant 0 \end{array} \right\} \qquad (5)$$

and
$$
\left.
\begin{aligned}
a_{11}x_1 + a_{12}x_2 + \ldots + a_{1n}x_n &\leq b_1 \\
a_{21}x_1 + a_{22}x_2 + \ldots + a_{2n}x_n &\leq b_2 \\
&\ \ \vdots \\
a_{m1}x_1 + a_{m2}x_2 + \ldots + a_{mn}x_n &\leq b_m
\end{aligned}
\right\} \quad (6)
$$

(cf. equations (1), (2) and (3))

Any problem which can be formulated as above, with $a_{11} \ldots a_{mn}$, $b_1 \ldots b_m$ and $c_1 \ldots c_n$ sets of constants and $x_1 \ldots x_n$ a set of variables, is a linear programming problem which may be solved by the Simplex method.

In the context of the preceding example,

n = no. of products produced

m = no. of machines required for their production

x_1 = no. of units of product 1 produced

x_2 = no. of units of product 2 produced

$\quad \cdot \qquad\qquad\qquad\quad \cdot$

$\quad \cdot \qquad\qquad\qquad\quad \cdot$

$\quad \cdot \qquad\qquad\qquad\quad \cdot$

x_n = no. of units of product n produced

c_1 = profit per unit on product 1

c_2 = profit per unit on product 2

$\quad \cdot \qquad\qquad\qquad\quad \cdot$

$\quad \cdot \qquad\qquad\qquad\quad \cdot$

$\quad \cdot \qquad\qquad\qquad\quad \cdot$

c_n = profit per unit on product n

b_1 = no. of hours available on machine 1

b_2 = no. of hours available on machine 2

$\quad \cdot \qquad\qquad\qquad\quad \cdot$

$\quad \cdot \qquad\qquad\qquad\quad \cdot$

$\quad \cdot \qquad\qquad\qquad\quad \cdot$

b_m = no. of hours available on machine m

a_{11} = no. of hours required on machine 1 by one unit of product 1

a_{12} = no. of hours required on machine 1 by one unit of product 2

a_{21} = no. of hours required on machine 2 by one unit of product 1

. .
. .
. .

a_{mn} = no. of hours required on machine m by one unit of product n.

Shadow prices

In addition to answering the question 'How much of each product should be produced in order to maximise profit?', the Simplex method also provides information on how much it would be worth paying for additional quantities of any resource. Consider a slightly modified version of Example 1, where the number of hours available on machine B is increased from 44 to 48. Fig. 7.4 shows the new feasible region.

Point Q (Fig. 7.4) represents, as before, the optimal solution to this problem, but the values of x_1 and x_2 corresponding to maximum

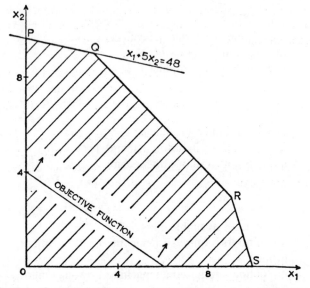

Fig. 7.4 Graphical solution to the modified version of Example 1

profit are now $x_1 = 3$, $x_2 = 9$. The new maximum profit is obtained by producing 3 units of product I and 9 units of product II and this profit is $(3 \times £6) + (9 \times £9)$ or £99. Thus, procuring 4 additional hours on machine B allows us to increase our profit by £3. It would be possible, therefore, to increase our net profit if we could obtain additional time on machine B at a cost of less than 75p per hour. This cost is known as the *shadow price* of the resource, machine B.

In a similar manner we could demonstrate that if we modified Example 1 by increasing the time available on machine A to 28 hours (the time on machine B remaining at 44 hours) the new maximum profit would be obtained by producing $6\frac{1}{2}$ units of product I and $7\frac{1}{2}$ units of product II giving a new profit of $(6\frac{1}{2} \times £6) + (7\frac{1}{2} \times £9)$ or £106·50. This results in a shadow price of £2·62$\frac{1}{2}$ per additional hour of the resource, machine A.

We should perhaps emphasise at this point that linear programming assumes that all units are infinitely divisible, such as is the case if a unit is a ton of material or a machine-hour. If this is not the case, and a unit is a component, for example, then an extension of linear programming, called *integer programming*, is required to give the best solution in terms of whole numbers.

As might be expected, increasing the number of hours available on machine C leads to no increase in profit. We do not even fully utilise the capacity we already have on this machine, and therefore the shadow price of the resource, machine C, is zero.

These shadow prices are produced as a by-product of the solution when the Simplex method is used. Without proof (which would take us beyond the scope of this book) we now demonstrate the calculations which lead to these shadow prices.

The two machines which are used to capacity in the optimum production plan are machines A and B. The equations which represent the utilisations of these machines, together with the profit function, are given below.

$$
\begin{array}{lll}
A & 2x_1 + 2x_2 = 24 & (7) \\
B & x_1 + 5x_2 = 44 & (8) \\
\text{Profit} & 6x_1 + 9x_2 &
\end{array}
$$

The optimum values of x_1 and x_2 are obtained by solving simultaneously equations (7) and (8). The shadow prices, on the other hand, are obtained by solving simultaneously new equations formed by considering the coefficients of x_1 and x_2 respectively. These coefficients appear in a vertical line in the expressions above and the equations are reproduced below:

$$2A + B = 6 \qquad \text{(coefficients of } x_1)$$
$$2A + 5B = 9 \qquad \text{(coefficients of } x_2)$$

Solving these equations simultaneously, we arrive at the shadow prices, $A = 2\cdot625$, $B = 0\cdot75$ as before. The shadow price of any resource not fully utilised is zero.

Before leaving the subject of shadow prices, we should mention that these prices are 'marginal' in the economist's use of the word. There comes a point beyond which additional time on machines A or B no longer increases the net profit by the above amounts. The ranges over which these shadow prices apply are found by an extension of linear programming called *parametric programming*.

There is an alternative formulation of the linear programming problem where the objective function is to be minimised instead of maximised. This is so, for instance, when the objective function is a cost rather than a profit. Exercise 3, at the end of the chapter, is such a minimisation problem. It is solved by the same Simplex method. The following example is also a minimisation problem – with rather special characteristics.

The transportation problem

The transportation problem is a linear programming problem for which there is a quicker method of solution than the more general Simplex method. The problem is one of selecting the optimum way of distributing a commodity from a number of despatch points to a number of destinations. The following is a typical example.

EXAMPLE 2

A company has four warehouses a, b, c and d. It is required to deliver a product from these warehouses to three customers, A, B and C. The warehouses have the following amounts in stock:

a	15 units
b	16 units
c	11 units
d	13 units
	55 units

The customers' requirements are:

A	17 units
B	20 units
C	18 units
	55 units

The costs of transporting one unit of the product from any warehouse *a*, *b*, *c* or *d*, to any customer *A*, *B* or *C* are given in Table 7.1.

The problem is to meet the customers' requirements whilst keeping the total transportation cost to a minimum.

Solution   The method of solution is to find, first, a feasible solution to the problem, i.e. a method of transporting the product which satisfies the customers' requirements whilst not violating the restrictions of availability. This solution is then tested to see whether it is the cheapest solution. If not, a cheaper solution is found, and retested in a similar manner. This process is repeated until no further reduction in cost is possible.

In the above example the number of units available equals the number required and hence any feasible solution meets each

Table 7.1   Transportation costs per unit (£)

Warehouses

		a	*b*	*c*	*d*
	A	8	9	6	3
Customers	*B*	6	11	5	10
	C	3	8	7	9

customer's requirement and leaves each warehouse empty. There are several ways of obtaining a feasible solution to the problem. A reasonable way is to allocate first as much as possible to that route having the least transportation cost per unit. There are two routes which have a unit transportation cost of £3. Let us start by allocating as much as possible to route dA. The maximum that can be allocated to this route is 13 – the amount initially held at warehouse d. Doing this leaves customer A requiring 4 units from any of the three remaining warehouses. The cheapest way customer A can receive these additional four units is from warehouse c – route cA having a unit transportation cost of £6. Allocating 4 units to this route satisfies customer A's requirement and reduces the amount held at warehouse c to 7 units. It is now cheaper to send the remaining 7 units at warehouse c to customer B than to customer C. Allocating 7 units to route cB exhausts the supply at warehouse c and reduces customer B's requirement from 20 units to 13. The cheapest way customer B can receive this amount is from warehouse a. Allocating 13 units to route aB satisfies customer B's requirement and reduces the amount at warehouse a, plus the 16 units at warehouse b, must finally go to customer C via routes aC and bC respectively. Table 7.2 illustrates this feasible solution. The question is 'Is it the minimum cost allocation?'

Table 7.2   Obtaining a feasible solution to Example 2

Warehouses

		a	b	c	d	Required	
	A	8	9	4 6	13 3	17	4
Customers	B	13 6	11	7 5	10	20	13
	C	2 3	16 8	7	9	18	
Available		15	16	11	13	55	
		2		7			

First let us determine the cost of transporting the product in this way. This is obtained by multiplying the cost of each route by the number of units transported along it, and summing for all routes as shown on the following pages.

Route	Cost/unit	No. of units	Cost/route
cA	£6	4	£24
dA	£3	13	£39
aB	£6	13	£78
cB	£5	7	£35
aC	£3	2	£6
bC	£8	16	£128

Total transportation cost £310

In order to see whether or not there is an alternative solution with a lower total transportation cost, we need to examine in turn each unused route to see whether or not the cost could be reduced by bringing it into use.

Consider the possibility of sending one unit along route *aA*. In order to achieve this, some modification to the remainder of the allocations is necessary. One unit must be subtracted from either of the routes *aB* or *aC* so that the restriction of there being only 15 units initially at warehouse *a* is not violated. If we reduce by one unit the amount sent along route *aB*, one unit must be added to route *cB* to maintain customer *B*'s requirement of 20. Finally, to comply with the restriction of only 11 units at warehouse *c*, one unit must be subtracted from route *cA*. This last subtraction compensates for the initial modification of sending one unit along the new route *aA* by maintaining customer *A*'s requirement of 17 units. These changes can be seen to have no effect on the feasibility of the initial allocation (see Table 7.3).

Table 7.3 Modification to the initial solution by bringing into use route *aA*

Warehouses

		a	b	c	d	Required
	A	$+1$ \ 8	9	4^{-1} \ 6	13 \ 3	17
Customers	B	13^{-1} \ 6	11	7^{+1} \ 5	10	20
	C	2 \ 3	16 \ 8	7	9	18
Available		15	16	11	13	55

The effect of the change is that customer A receives one more unit from warehouse a and one less from warehouse c, whilst customer B receives one more from c and one less from a. The former has the effect of increasing the transportation cost by £2 – the unit cost of route aA being £8 compared with £6 of route cA – whilst the latter reduces the transportation cost by £1. The net result is that the modified solution shows an increase rather than a decrease in the total transportation cost.

If c_{aA} is the unit transportation cost from warehouse a to customer A, c_{bA} is the unit transportation cost from warehouse b to customer A, etc., the change in cost in the above modification is given by $c_{aA} - c_{cA} + c_{cB} - c_{aB}$. This equals £8 − £6 + £5 − £6, i.e. £1. A positive sign represents an increase in cost whilst a negative sign represents a decrease.

The above inspection procedure could be repeated for each unused route in turn to test whether or not the initial solution can be improved. A short cut to this rather laborious method is provided by the concept of *shadow costs*. Shadow costs are obtained by assuming that the transportation cost for all used routes is made up of two parts – a cost of despatch, a, b, c or d and a cost of reception, A, B or C – such that the unit cost $c_{cA} = c + A$, $c_{dA} = d + A$, etc. Under this assumption, by assigning an arbitrary value to one of the shadow costs, for example A, the remaining ones, a, b, c, d, B and C may be uniquely determined provided that the solution employs exactly six routes, i.e. one route for each shadow cost required. The initial allocation does use exactly six routes and therefore the shadow costs may be determined from the following six equations:

$$c + A = 6, d + A = 3, a + B = 6, c + B = 5,$$
$$a + C = 3, \text{ and } b + C = 8$$

If A is made equal to zero, these equations may be solved to give $a = 7$, $b = 12$, $c = 6$, $d = 3$, $B = -1$, and $C = -4$. Table 7.4 shows, along with the initial allocation, these shadow costs.

We showed previously how introducing the route aA into the solution, and sending one unit along it, increased the total transportation cost by $c_{aA} - c_{cA} + c_{cB} - c_{aB}$. In terms of shadow costs this is equivalent to

$$c_{aA} - (c + A) + (c + B) - (a + B),$$

Table 7.4 Shadow costs

Warehouses

		a	b	c	d	
	Shadow costs	7	12	6	3	Required
A	0	8	9	4 ⁶	13 ³	17
B	−1	13 ⁶	11	7 ⁵	10	20
C	−4	2 ³	16 ⁸	7	9	18
Available		15	16	11	13	55

Customers label appears to the left of the rows A, B, C. The small corner numbers are: A row — a:8, b:9, c:6, d:3; B row — a:6, b:11, c:5, d:10; C row — a:3, b:8, c:7, d:9. The main-cell values are: A: c = 4, d = 13; B: a = 13, c = 7; C: a = 2, b = 16.

which simplifies to $c_{aA} - (a + A)$. This illustrates a general result, that the sending of one unit along a previously unoccupied route increases the total transportation cost by the unit transportation cost of the new route minus the sum of the shadow costs for that route. Thus if this difference is negative for any unused route, a saving in cost, equal to this difference, will be made for each unit that can be transferred to this route. We can now evaluate this difference for each unused route in the initial allocation as follows:

$$c_{aA} - (a + A) = 8 - (7 + 0) = 1$$

(This confirms the previous analysis of this route.)

$$c_{bA} - (b + A) = 9 - (12 + 0) = -3$$
$$c_{bB} - (b + B) = 11 - (12 - 1) = 0$$
$$c_{dB} - (d + B) = 10 - (3 - 1) = 8$$
$$c_{cC} - (c + C) = 7 - (6 - 4) = 5$$
$$c_{dC} - (d + C) = 9 - (3 - 4) = 10$$

These results are entered in the top left-hand corner of the appropriate squares in Table 7.5.

Table 7.5 Difference between unit transportation cost and sum of shadow costs for unused routes

Warehouses

		a	b	c	d	Required
	Shadow costs	7	12	6	3	*Required*
A	0	(1) ⠀⠀8	(−3) ⠀⠀9	4 ⠀⠀6	13 ⠀⠀3	17
B	−1	13 ⠀⠀6	(0) ⠀⠀11	7 ⠀⠀5	(8) ⠀⠀10	20
C	−4	2 ⠀⠀3	16 ⠀⠀8	(5) ⠀⠀7	(10) ⠀⠀9	18

Customers (label at left of rows)

| Available | 15 | 16 | 11 | 13 | 55 |

We note that a saving of £3 can be made for each unit that can be sent along route bA. The next step is to utilise this new route as fully as possible whilst still satisfying the movement requirements. Table 7.6 illustrates how this is achieved.

Assume we send x units along route bA. In order not to exceed the number initially held at warehouse b, the number sent along route bC must be reduced to $16 - x$. However, this reduces by x the number of units sent to customer C, and so the amount sent along route aC must be increased to $2 + x$ units. By a similar chain of reasoning the numbers sent along routes aB, cB and cA are seen to be $13 - x$, $7 + x$ and $4 - x$ respectively. Reference to Table 7.6 will show that this modification in no way affects the feasibility of the solution, provided that x is not so large that any route allocation becomes negative. The value of x is actually chosen so that the amount sent along one of the previously used routes falls to zero. This occurs along route cA when x takes the value 4. Substituting 4 for x in Table 7.6 yields the improved solution of Table 7.7.

Sending 4 items along a route whose potential saving is £3 per unit reduces the total transportation cost by £12. This saving may be verified by evaluating the new total transportation cost as follows:

Route	Cost/unit	No. of unit	Cost/route
bA	£9	4	£36
dA	£3	13	£39
aB	£6	9	£54
cB	£5	11	£55
aC	£3	6	£18
bC	£8	12	£96
		Total transportation cost	£298

Table 7.6 Utilising a new route as fully as possible

Warehouses

		a	b	c	d	
	Shadow costs	7	12	6	3	Required
A	0	(1) 8	(−3) +x 9	4^{-x} 6	13 3	17
B	−1	13^{-x} 6	(0) 11	7^{+x} 5	(8) 10	20
C	−4	2^{+x} 3	16^{-x} 8	(5) 7	(10) 9	18
Available		15	16	11	13	55

Customers (left of B row)

Table 7.7 Second feasible solution

Warehouses

		a	b	c	d	Required
	A	8	4 9	6	13 3	17
Customers	B	9 6	11	11 5	10	20
	C	6 3	12 8	7	9	18
	Available	15	16	11	13	55

In order to determine whether further improvement to the solution is possible, new shadow costs are calculated for the second feasible solution and the test procedure repeated. This reiterative process is continued until no further improvement is possible. In practice, all the calculations necessary within an iteration can be carried out using one table – Table 7.6 – constructed via Tables 7.2, 7.4 and 7.5. The second iteration of the present problem is illustrated in Table 7.8.

Table 7.8 Second iteration of Example 2

			Warehouses				
			a	*b*	*c*	*d*	
		Shadow costs	4	9	3	3	*Required*
Customers	*A*	0	(4) 8	4 9	(3) 6	13 3	17
	B	2	9 6	(0) 11	11 5	(5) 10	20
	C	−1	6 3	12 8	(5) 7	(7) 9	18
Available			15	16	11	13	55

Arbitrarily assigning the value of zero to shadow cost A, the new shadow costs, a, b, c, d, B and C, obtained by solving the following equations:

$$b + A = 9, d + A = 3, a + B = 6, c + B = 5,$$
$$a + C = 3, \text{ and } b + C = 8$$

are 4, 9, 3, 3, 2 and −1 respectively. Also, the differences between the unit transportation costs and the sum of the shadow costs for the unused routes, aA, cA, bB, dB, cC and dC, are 4, 3, 0, 5, 5 and 7. None is negative, and therefore no further improvement to the solution is possible. The minimum cost allocation is £298.

It is interesting to note at this point the significance of a zero difference between the unit transportation cost and the sum of the shadow costs – as is the case for the unused route bB. By definition, the bringing into use of such a route will cause neither an increase nor a decrease in the total transportation cost. Hence, when a difference of zero exists in the optimal solution, this solution is not unique. The reader may like to verify for himself that the sending of any number up to 9 units along route dB (with the necessary adjustment to the amounts sent along routes aB, aC and bC) does not affect the total transportation cost.

In the previous example we indicated that shadow costs could always be found, provided that the solution to be tested employs six routes, i.e. one less than the combined number of warehouses and customers. It can be shown, quite generally, that in order to determine shadow costs uniquely, the solution to be tested must employ exactly $m + n - 1$ routes, where m is the number of despatch points and n the number of destinations. If a feasible solution uses less than this number of routes, we say that such a solution is 'degenerate'. How a degenerate solution can arise, and the computational device for overcoming the difficulty, is illustrated in the next example. Before proceeding to Example 3, the reader may like to verify that the transportation problem is a linear programming problem by attempting the standard linear programming formulation of the previous example. This formulation is given on page 224.

EXAMPLE 3

Consider a problem similar to that of Example 2, where the customers' requirements are changed to the following:

$$
\begin{array}{ll}
A & 19 \text{ units} \\
B & 12 \text{ units} \\
C & 14 \text{ units} \\
\hline
& 45 \text{ units} \\
\hline
\end{array}
$$

The amounts at the four warehouses and the unit transportation costs are unchanged.

Solution   The first point to notice is that the number of units available no longer equals the number required. However, the demand can be matched to the supply by postulating the existence of a fourth customer, D – a 'dummy' customer – whose requirement is 10 units, the transportation cost from any warehouse to the dummy customer being zero.

We can now adopt the procedure of Example 2 to find a first feasible solution. Because of the existence of the dummy customer there are four routes having a transportation cost of zero. In this case, it is usually a good plan to allocate as much as possible to that route connecting the dummy customer with the warehouse from which the highest transportation costs arise. The transportation costs from warehouse b tend to be higher than those from the other warehouses and so we allocate, initially, as much as possible to route bD. Following the initial procedure of Example 2 leads eventually to the feasible solution of Table 7.9.

Table 7.9   Obtaining a feasible solution to Example 3

Warehouses

		a	b	c	d	Required	
	A	8	9	6 ₍6₎	13 ₍3₎	~~19~~	13
Customers	B	7 ₍6₎	11	5 ₍5₎	10	~~12~~	5
	C	8 ₍3₎	6 ₍8₎	7	9	~~14~~	8
	D	0	10 ₍0₎	0	0	10	
Available		~~15~~	~~16~~	~~11~~	~~13~~	55	
		7	6	6			

There are $m + n - 1$ routes employed in this solution and therefore shadow costs can be found in order to test whether any improvement is possible. The differences between the transportation cost and the sum of the shadow costs for the unused routes are given in Table 7.10. Utilising route bA – the only route with a negative difference – as fully as possible, involves sending 6 units

Table 7.10 Differences indicating potentialities of unused routes

		Warehouses				
		a	*b*	*c*	*d*	
	Shadow costs	7	12	6	3	*Required*
A	0	(1) / 8	(−3) x / 9	6^{-x} / 6	13 / 3	19
B	−1	7^{-x} / 6	(0) / 11	5^{+x} / 5	(8) / 10	12
C	−4	8^{+x} / 3	6^{-x} / 8	(5) / 7	(10) / 9	14
D	−12	(5) / 0	10 / 0	(6) / 0	(9) / 0	10
Available		15	16	11	13	55

Customers

along it (see Table 7.10). Notice, however, that whilst one new route comes into use, *two* old ones go out of use, resulting in a new feasible solution employing only $m + n - 2$ routes (see Table 7.11). It is now impossible to determine the seven shadow costs, $a, b, c, d,$

Table 7.11 Second feasible solution employing $m + n - 2$ routes

	Warehouses				
	a	*b*	*c*	*d*	*Required*
A	8	6 / 9	6	13 / 3	19
B	1 / 6	11	11 / 5	10	12
C	14 / 3	8	7	9	14
D	0	10 / 0	0	0	10
Available	15	16	11	13	55

Customers

B, *C* and *D* under these conditions. This difficulty is overcome by allocating a very small amount, ε, to one of the unused routes. This is purely a computational device for converting an unused route into a used one. It does not materially affect the allocation, but it does allow all the shadow costs to be calculated so that any possible improvement to the solution may be discovered.

In our present example we allow the new route *bA* to replace only one of the previously used routes, for example *bC*, the other route *cA* remaining in the solution at 'zero level'. We can now test whether any improvement on this solution is possible. Table 7.12

Table 7.12   Second iteration using one route at 'zero level'

		Warehouse				
		a	*b*	*c*	*d*	
	Shadow costs	7	9	6	3	*Required*
A	0	(1) 8	6 9	ε 6	13 3	19
B	−1	1 6	(3) 11	11 5	(8) 10	12
C	−4	14 3	(3) 8	(5) 7	(10) 9	14
D	−9	(2) 0	10 0	(3) 0	(6) 0	10
Available		15	16	11	13	55

(*Customers* labels the row group *A*, *B*, *C*, *D*.)

shows that no difference is negative and therefore the present allocation is the optimal one. The ε, having served its purpose, may now be ignored. Discarding also the concept of the dummy customer, we find that the excess of supply over demand remains at warehouse *b*.

The total transportation cost is given below.

Route	Cost/unit	No. of units	Cost/route
bA	£9	6	£54
dA	£3	13	£39
aB	£6	1	£6
cB	£5	11	£55
aC	£3	14	£42

Total transportation cost £196

The use of the transportation technique is not restricted to problems involving the physical transportation of items from despatch points to destinations. The following is a production scheduling problem which permits an identical method of solution.

EXAMPLE 4

A manufacturer has to satisfy the following demand for his product during a six-month period:

January	1000 items
February	1400 items
March	1600 items
April	2100 items
May	2500 items
June	4000 items

The production capacity allows a maximum of 2000 items to be produced in any month under normal working conditions, with the possibility of an additional 500 items if overtime is worked. The cost per item of producing the product in normal time is £12. This cost is increased to £12·60 for those items produced during overtime. Goods not sold during the month of manufacture may be stored for sale in succeeding months – the storage charges being 20% per annum of the production costs. How many items should be manufactured each month in order to minimise the sum of the production and storage costs?

Solution The problem may be formulated as a transportation problem. The goods produced each month within normal time and overtime are the amounts available – this corresponds to twelve despatch points – and the monthly demands are the amounts required. As in the previous example, a dummy customer is introduced to represent the unused capacity, thus giving a total of seven destinations. The cost of producing and selling an item in the same month is simply the unit production cost. The cost of producing an item in one month and selling it in a succeeding month is the sum of the production and storage costs. Because no shortages are allowed, demand in one month cannot be met from any succeeding month's production; hence a prohibitively large cost M is assigned to such practice. The cost of supplying the dummy customer is, of course, zero.

The storage cost is easily obtained: for items produced during normal hours this is 20% of £12 per annum or 20p per month, whilst for items produced during overtime the corresponding monthly cost is 21p.

The total demand over the 6-month period is 12 600 items. Normal time and overtime capacities are sufficient for 12 000 and 3000 items respectively and so 2400 units of capacity remain unused. By definition, overtime is not worked until the normal time for any month is fully utilised.

In order to arrive at a first feasible solution, we follow the procedure of Example 3 and allocate as much as possible to those 'routes' with zero cost, commencing with the column where the average cost is greatest. Thus we allocate 500 items to the 'overtime–excess capacity' routes of January, February, March and April and 400 items to the overtime–excess capacity route of May. Proceeding stepwise from this point we arrive at the solution of Table 7.13. The cost of this schedule is £153 160. This is not the optimal solution, however, and the reader may like to verify that successive iterations reduce the cost to £153 140 and finally to £153 080, yielding the degenerate solution of Table 7.14.

The optimum production schedule is as follows:

January	1600 items
February	2000 items
March	2000 items
April	2000 items
May	2500 items
June	2500 items

Table 7.13 Formulation and first feasible solution of production scheduling problem

Sales month	January Normal-time	January Over-time	February Normal-time	February Over-time	March Normal-time	March Over-time	April Normal-time	April Over-time	May Normal-time	May Over-time	June Normal-time	June Over-time	Required
January	1000 / 12.00	/ 12.60	M	M	M	M	M	M	M	M	M	M	~~1000~~
February	/ 12.20	/ 12.81	1400 / 12.00	/ 12.60	M	M	M	M	M	M	M	M	~~1400~~
March	/ 12.40	/ 13.02	100 / 12.20	/ 12.81	1500 / 12.00	/ 12.60	M	M	M	M	M	M	~~1600~~ ~~100~~
April	/ 12.60	/ 13.23	/ 12.40	/ 13.02	500 / 12.20	/ 12.81	1600 / 12.00	500 / 12.60	M	M	M	M	~~2100~~ ~~500~~
May	/ 12.80	/ 13.44	/ 12.60	/ 13.23	/ 12.40	/ 13.02	400 / 12.20	/ 12.81	2000 / 12.00	100 / 12.60	M	M	~~2500~~ ~~2400~~ ~~400~~
June	1000 / 13.00	/ 13.65	500 / 12.80	/ 13.44	/ 12.60	/ 13.23	/ 12.40	/ 13.02	/ 12.20	/ 12.81	2000 / 12.00	500 / 12.60	~~4000~~ ~~3500~~ ~~1000~~
Excess capacity	/ 0	500 / 0	/ 0	500 / 0	/ 0	500 / 0	/ 0	500 / 0	/ 0	400 / 0	/ 0	/ 0	~~2400~~ ~~1900~~ ~~900~~
Available	~~2000~~ ~~1000~~	500	~~2000~~ ~~1900~~ ~~500~~	500	~~2000~~ ~~1500~~	500	~~2000~~ ~~1600~~	500	2000	~~500~~ ~~100~~	2000	500	15 000

Production month (column headings) / *Sales month* (row headings)

Table 7.14 Minimum cost solution of production scheduling problem

Sales month (rows) × Production month (columns)

Sales month	January		February		March		April		May		June		Required
	Normal time	Over-time	Normal time	Over-time	Normal time	Over-time	Normal time	Over-time	Normal time	Over-time	Normal time	Over-time	
January	1000 / 12.00	M / 12.60	M	M	M	M	M	M	M	M	M	M	1000
February	12.20	12.80	1400 / 12.00	M / 12.60	M	M	M	M	M	M	M	M	1400
March	12.40	13.00	12.20	12.80	1600 / 12.00	M / 12.60	M	M	M	M	M	M	1600
April	12.60	13.23	12.40	13.02	400 / 12.20	M / 12.81	1700 / 12.00	M / 12.60	M	M	M	M	2100
May	12.80	13.44	12.60	13.23	12.40	13.02	12.20	12.81	2000 / 12.00	500 / 12.60	M	M	2500
June	600 / 13.00	13.65	600 / 12.80	13.44	12.60	13.23	300 / 12.40	13.02	12.20	12.81	2000 / 12.00	500 / 12.60	4000
Excess capacity	400 / 0	500 / 0	0	500 / 0	0	500 / 0	0	500 / 0	0	0	0	0	2400
Available	2000	500	2000	500	2000	500	2000	500	2000	500	2000	500	15 000

The discerning reader may observe that the solution of Table 7.14 is not unique. In fact, if the items are produced as above it does not matter when they are sold, the total cost will remain the same. The reason for this is that the storage cost increases linearly with time, i.e. it costs twice as much to store an item two months as to store it one month. There are situations, however, where, because of the risk of deterioration or obsolescence, the monthly storage cost increases as the duration of storage increases. The transportation model does not preclude the use of any storage cost provided it can be quantified. If we had assumed that the interest charges on capital tied up in stock were compounded monthly, a 'first-in first-out' stores policy would have resulted, giving the following production and sales plan.

	Production	*Sales*
January	1600	1000 in January
		600 in February
February	2000	800 in February
		1200 in March
March	2000	400 in March
		1600 in April
April	2000	500 in April
		1500 in May
May	2500	1000 in May
		1500 in June
June	2500	2500 in June

Even this solution is not unique. An alternative is to produce only 1100 items in January and work overtime, producing 2500 items in April. It is interesting to note that, although this alternative solution is equally optimal, a manager would invariably choose the former solution. Why is this? The most probable answer lies in our assumption that excess capacity during normal working hours costs nothing. In practice, however, it is impossible to lay off all the labour concerned with production for several weeks. Attaching a suitable cost to this excess capacity may well alter the production policy significantly. Another reason for choosing the former solution is that, if the requirements (which are usually only forecasts) underestimate the actual demand, producing only 1100 items in January may mean that there is not enough capacity, even working overtime, to meet later demands. Methods are currently being developed for the solution of transportation problems where the requirements and capacities are expressed not as fixed values but in the form of probability distributions.

Although the computational procedure for transportation problems is basically simple, the manual solution of problems with many despatch points and many destinations soon becomes laborious. As is the case for the Simplex method, standard computer programs are available for the transportation routine.

The assignment problem

A special form of the transportation problem occurs when there is just one item at each of several despatch points and one item is required at each of several destinations. The problem here is to assign the items to the destinations in an optimal manner, and we speak of this as an assignment problem.

EXAMPLE 5

A car hire company has one car at each of five depots a, b, c, d and e. A customer in each of the five towns A, B, C, D and E requires a car. The distances, between the depots and the towns where the customers are, are given in Table 7.15.

Table 7.15 Distances between depots and customers (kilometres)

	a	b	c	d	e
A	160	130	175	190	200
B	135	120	130	160	175
C	140	110	155	170	185
D	50	50	80	80	110
E	55	35	70	80	105

How should the cars be assigned to the customers so as to minimise the distance travelled?

Solution This problem could be solved using the transportation technique. However, only five of the routes will be used and so an additional four routes would have to be included at zero level in order to determine shadow costs and thus test for optimality. Because of the special characteristics of this class of problem, a different approach is more useful. The problem is to select five elements from the matrix of Table 7.15 such that there is one element in each row, one in each column, and the sum is the minimum possible.

Clearly to enumerate all possibilities – there are 120 of them – would be tedious, and out of the question in a larger problem. We may simplify the problem, however, by noting the following important result:

Subtracting (or adding) any number from (or to) every element in a row or column does not affect the optimal assignment.

Suppose, for instance, we subtract 10 from each element in the first row of Table 7.15. As one, and only one, element of this row appears in the optimal assignment, the only effect of this is to decrease by 10 the total distance travelled. Thus the assignment which minimises the distance travelled in the original problem automatically minimises the distance in the revised problem.

Table 7.16 First modification to matrix of Table 7.15

	a	b	c	d	e
A	30	0	45	60	70
B	15	0	10	40	55
C	30	0	45	60	75
D	0	0	30	30	60
E	20	0	35	45	70

The method of solution, therefore, is as follows:

Step 1: Subtract the smallest element in each row from every element in that row. This yields the new matrix of distances as shown on Table 7.16.

Step 2: Subtract the smallest element in each column of Table 7.16 from every element in that column. This yields the following distance matrix:

Table 7.17　Second modification to matrix of Table 7.15

	a	b	c	d	e
A	30	0	35	30	15
B	15	0	0	10	0
C	30	0	35	30	20
D	0	0	20	0	5
E	20	0	25	15	15

Step 3: Test whether it is possible to make an assignment using only zero distances. If this is possible, clearly the assignment must be an optimal one, since no element in the matrix of Table 7.17 is negative. It can be shown that a 'zero assignment' can only be made if the minimum number of horizontal and vertical lines necessary to cover all zeros in the matrix equals the number of rows in the matrix – 5 in this case. Applying this test to the matrix of Table 7.17 we find that three lines, suitably chosen, cover all zeros (see Table 7.18). Thus a zero assignment is not possible at this stage.

Step 4:
  (i) Find the smallest uncovered element as a result of Step 3. Call this element x.
  (ii) Subtract x from every element in the matrix.

Table 7.18 The minimum number of lines which cover all the zeros of Table 7.17

	a	b	c	d	e
A	30	0	35	30	15
B	15	0	0	10	0
C	30	0	35	30	20
D	0	0	20	0	5
E	20	0	25	15	15

(iii) Re-add x to every element in all rows and columns covered by lines.
(iv) Re-apply the test of Step 3 to the resulting matrix.

The effect of (ii) and (iii) above is to:

Subtract x from all uncovered elements, add x to elements at the intersection of two lines, and leave unchanged elements covered by one line.

Applying Step 4 to the matrix of Table 7.17 we note that $x = 15$ and get the results in Table 7.19. The zeros in this matrix cannot be

Table 7.19 Third modification to matrix of Table 7.15

	a	b	c	d	e
A	15	0	20	15	0
B	15	15	0	10	0
C	15	0	20	15	5
D	0	15	20	0	5
E	5	0	10	0	0

covered by fewer than five lines and hence a zero assignment is now possible. This is indicated below:

Table 7.20   Optimal assignment for Example 5

	a	b	c	d	e
A	15	Ø	20	15	**0**
B	15	15	**0**	10	Ø
C	15	**0**	20	15	5
D	**0**	15	20	Ø	5
E	5	Ø	10	**0**	Ø

To reach this assignment we proceed as follows:

Columns 1 and 3 each contain only one zero. These zeros must, therefore, form part of the optimal assignment and are indicated in bold type. The additional zeros in rows 2 and 4 can now be crossed out as they cannot feature in the final assignment. This leaves column 4 with one zero remaining. This is indicated in bold type, the two other zeros in row 5 are crossed out. Column 5 now has one zero remaining and, when this is eliminated, the zero at the intersection of row 3 and column 2 completes the assignment.

The minimum assignment is therefore:

Route	Distance
aD	50 kilometres
bC	110
cB	130
dE	80
eA	200

Total distance travelled: 570 kilometres

The above procedure may be used to determine the optimal assignment in any situation where the effectiveness of the pairings of two sets of data may be measured. For example, a department

head may have a number of jobs and an equal number of subordinates who would carry out the jobs. The problem of how to assign the
subordinates to the jobs to minimise the time taken, or maximise
the effectiveness of the staff, is only a simple variation of the
preceding problem. A 'maximisation' problem may be converted
into a 'minimisation' one by the initial step of subtracting each
element of the matrix from the largest element in the matrix.

Mathematical programming

The preceding five examples chosen to illustrate linear programming have necessarily been simple. Their object was to indicate that
class of problem to which linear programming is relevant. One point
which must be borne in mind is that a solution obtained by linear
programming cannot be more accurate than the data on which it is
based and, as with many other techniques, one value of the formulation of the problem is to highlight those quantities of resources,
costs, etc. which need to be accurately determined before an
optimal solution can be found.

There are techniques of mathematical programming, many of
which are developments from linear programming, to handle systems that do not have linear properties (see bibliography). These
involve a considerable increase in the amount of calculation required to find an optimal solution, and the cost of the computer time
involved may be justified only for very extensive systems. In some
cases the collection of data (other than that on policy decisions), the
calculation of the optimal allocation of resources, and the imple-
mentation of the decision have been done entirely automatically.

Exercises

7.1 A toy company manufactures two types of doll; a basic version
– doll *A* – and a de luxe version – doll *B*. Each doll of type *B*
takes twice as long to produce as one of type *A*, and the
company would have time to make a maximum of 2000 per day
if it produced only the basic version. The supply of plastic is
sufficient to produce 1500 dolls per day (both *A* and *B*
combined). The de luxe version requires a fancy dress of which
there are only 600 per day available. If the company makes a

profit of £3 and £5 per doll, respectively, on dolls A and B, how many of each should be produced per day in order to maximise profit?

7.2 A factory manufactures two qualities of tweed. 1 metre of tweed A requires 160 grams of grey wool, 50 grams of red wool and 40 grams of green wool, whilst 1 metre of tweed B is made up of 200 grams of grey wool, 20 grams of red wool and 80 grams of green wool. The amounts of wool available in a given period are 1600 kg of grey, 400 kg of red and 600 kg of green. Both tweeds can be produced on the same machines and both can be woven at a rate of 12 metres per hour. A total of 750 machine hours are available in the given period. The profit per metre is £2 for tweed A and £4 for tweed B.

(a) Given that the company has firm orders for, and is obliged to produce, at least 3000 metres of tweed A, how much of each should be manufactured in order to maximise profit?

(b) By how much would the profit be increased if the necessity to produce at least 3000 metres of tweed A were relaxed?

7.3 A diet is required which will provide an animal with 3000 calories and 80 units of protein per day. There are four basic foods which may be used in preparing the diet. Food I costs 40p per kg, food II 20p per kg, food III 50p per kg and food IV 60p per kg.

food I	contains	600	calories and	2	units of protein;
food II	,,	50	,,	,,	8	,,	,,	,,	;
food III	,,	500	,,	,,	10	,,	,,	,,	;
and food IV	,,	800	,,	,,	3	,,	,,	,,	.

Formulate the problem of determining the cheapest food combination that will satisfy the diet requirement.

7.4 Three depots, *a*, *b* and *c*, have the following buses available:

a	1 bus
b	8 buses
c	7 buses
	16 buses

These buses are required at three termini, *A*, *B* and *C*, as follows:

A	2 buses
B	5 buses
C	9 buses
	16 buses

The distances, in kilometres, between the depots and the termini are given in the table below:

	a	*b*	*c*
A	6	10	15
B	4	6	16
C	12	5	8

How should the buses be allocated to the termini so that the total distance travelled is a minimum?

7.5 Fig. 7.5 represents a railway network. The points labelled *a*, *b*, *c* and *d* represent collieries and those labelled *A*, *B* and *C* represent the coke ovens of a steelworks. The rail distances (kilometres) from these points to the junctions of the network, and from one junction to another, are shown by the numbers on the lines.

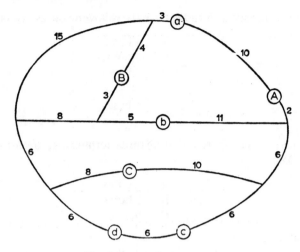

Fig. 7.5   A railway network

The collieries can supply the following amounts:

a	3000 tons/month
b	2000 tons/month
c	8000 tons/month
d	3000 tons/month

The requirements for the coke ovens are:

A	2000 tons/month
B	4000 tons/month
C	6000 tons/month

If the transportation cost is 5p per ton-kilometre, find that distribution of coal from the collieries to coke ovens which minimises the total transportation cost.

What is the minimum cost per month?

7.6   A head of department has five jobs *A*, *B*, *C*, *D* and *E* and five subordinates, *V*, *W*, *X*, *Y* and *Z*, who are capable of carrying out the jobs. He assesses the number of hours each man would take to perform each job as follows:

	V	W	X	Y	Z
A	3	5	10	15	8
B	4	7	15	18	8
C	8	12	20	20	12
D	5	5	8	10	6
E	10	10	15	25	10

How should the jobs be allocated to the men to minimise the total time taken?

7.7 Write out the complete linear programming formulation for question 6 (above).

8

Theory of Games

Introduction

Many decisions have to be taken in a competitive situation where the outcome depends not on this decision alone but rather on the interaction between this decision and that of a competitor. The term 'game' used in this chapter is not simply confined to recreational activities, but embraces all competitive decision-making situations, including the most serious of all – war. Indeed it was not a coincidence that the classic work on the theory of games by von Neumann and Morgenstern was first published during the Second World War.

Many competitive business situations are too complex for the theory, in its present stage of development, to solve. Nevertheless, a knowledge of the concepts involved in the theory, particularly the importance of the role of chance, helps to clarify the issues involved in many decision-making situations.

A competitive situation is called a game if it has, for example, the following properties:

(a) There are a finite number of participants, called *players*.
(b) Each player has a finite number of possible *courses of action*.
(c) *A play* occurs when each player chooses one of his courses of action. (The choices are assumed to be made simultaneously, i.e., no player knows the choice of another until he has decided on his own.)
(d) Every combination of courses of action determines an *out-*

come which results in a gain to each player. (A loss is considered a negative gain.)

The simplest type of game is one which has only two players, and where the gain of one is the loss of the other. Such a game is called a *zero-sum two-person game*.

The gains resulting from a zero-sum two-person game are most easily represented in the form of a matrix, known as the *pay-off matrix*. An example of such a matrix is given below.

$$\begin{array}{c} & & \textit{Player B} \\ & & \begin{array}{cccc} \text{I} & \text{II} & \text{III} & \text{IV} \end{array} \\ \textit{Player A} & \begin{array}{c} \text{I} \\ \text{II} \\ \text{III} \end{array} & \begin{bmatrix} 6 & 0 & -2 & -5 \\ 3 & 2 & 1 & 3 \\ -1 & 1 & 0 & 4 \end{bmatrix} \end{array}$$

The number of rows of the matrix correspond to the number of courses of action of player A, and the number of columns correspond to the number of courses of action of player B. The elements within the matrix represent the gain to player A for each outcome of the game; thus a positive entry indicates a payment from B to A whilst a negative entry denotes a payment from A to B. For example, if player A uses his third course of action and player B uses his first, A pays B one unit.

The *strategy* of a player is the decision rule he uses to decide which course of action he should employ. This strategy may be of two kinds:

(*a*) A *pure strategy* is a decision always to select the same course of action.

(*b*) A *mixed strategy* is a decision to choose at least two of his courses of action with fixed probabilities; i.e. if a player decides to use just two courses of action with equal probability, he might spin a coin to decide which one to choose. The advantage of a mixed strategy is that an opponent is always kept guessing as to which course of action is to be selected on any particular occasion.

The *value* of a game is the expected gain of player A if both players use their best strategies. We define 'best strategy' on the basis of the *minimax criterion of optimality*. This states that if a player lists the worst possible outcomes of all his potential strategies, he will choose that strategy which corresponds to the best of these worst outcomes. The implication of this criterion is that the opponent is an extremely shrewd player who will ensure that, whatever our strategy, our gain is kept to a minimum.

The *solution* of a game involves finding:

(*a*) The best strategies for both players.
(*b*) The value of the game.

It is a feature of the solution that the situation where both players use their best strategies is stable, in the sense that neither player can increase his gain by deviating from his initial strategy once he becomes aware of his opponent's.

Saddle points

The simplest type of game is one where the best strategies for both players are pure strategies. This is the case if, and only if, the pay-off matrix contains a saddle point. A saddle point is an element of the matrix which is both the smallest element in its row and the largest element in its column. We shall see why pure strategies are the best strategies in this case by reference to Example 1.

EXAMPLE 1
The pay-off matrix for a zero-sum two-person game is given below. Find the best strategy for each player and the value of the game.

		Player B				
		I	II	III	IV	V
	I	-2	0	0	5	3
Player A	II	3	2	1	2	2
	III	-4	-3	0	-2	6
	IV	5	3	-4	2	-6

Solution   On examining each of his pure strategies player *A* notes that the worst outcome if he plays his course of action I throughout occurs when B also plays I and the resulting gain to *A* is -2. Similarly the worst outcomes when *A* plays II, III and IV are 1, -4 and -6 respectively. Player *A*, therefore, can guarantee a gain of at least 1 by using his course of action II throughout.

Looking now at the game from the point of view of player B; his worst outcomes, taking each pure strategy in turn, are 5, 3, 1, 5 and 6. (NB. As the entries in the matrix represent gains to A, the larger the entry the more unfavourable the result is to B.) Player B can guarantee a loss of at most 1 by using his strategy III throughout.

If A can guarantee a minimum gain of 1, B cannot have a better strategy than one which precludes A from gaining more than 1. Similarly, if B can guarantee a maximum loss of 1, A's best strategy is that which ensures that B loses no less than 1.

The solution is, therefore:

Player A uses his course of action II throughout.
Player B uses his course of action III throughout.

The value of the game is 1.

The solution is stable, in that when player A realises that B is playing III throughout he cannot afford to change his own strategy, 1 being the largest element in column III. For similar reasons B has no incentive to change his initial strategy when he discovers how A is playing.

It will be noticed from Example 1 that a saddle point occurs when the element which is the largest of the row minima equals the element which is the smallest of the column maxima. The solution of such a game lies in player A choosing consistently that course of action corresponding to the row through the saddle point and player B choosing always that course of action corresponding to the column through the saddle point. The element at the saddle point determines the value of the game.

Mixed strategies

A stable solution can only exist in terms of pure strategies when the pay-off matrix has a saddle point.

If there is no such saddle point the best strategies are mixed strategies and the problem becomes one of evaluating the probabilities with which each course of action should be selected.

Consider the following game of Matching Pennies. Two players, A and B, each put down a penny. If the coins match, i.e. both are heads or both are tails, A collects them both; otherwise B collects them both. The pay-off matrix for this game is given below:

Player B

		I (Heads)	II (Tails)
Player A	I (Heads)	1	−1
	II (Tails)	−1	1

Intuitively, it can be seen that it is not a good plan for either player to decide in advance to play either of his pure strategies. Success in this game lies in attempting to anticipate the opposing player's course of action. A player could score over his opponent if he detected any pattern in his opponent's strategy or noticed that his opponent had a preference for either heads or tails. The opponent may only obviate such detection by selecting his courses of action at random such that the probability of choosing either heads or tails is $\frac{1}{2}$. Such a strategy may be represented as $(\frac{1}{2}, \frac{1}{2})$. A player may employ this strategy, for example, by tossing the coin. If player A used this strategy he would win, on average, as often as he would lose, and his average or expected gain would be zero. This would be true whatever strategy player B adopted, whether he played heads throughout, tails throughout, or used the same strategy as A. If player A uses the strategy $(\frac{1}{2}, \frac{1}{2})$ he cannot lose whatever B decides to do. Similar reasoning also holds for player B. As there is no strategy for either player which will ensure a positive gain, the strategy $(\frac{1}{2}, \frac{1}{2})$ is the optimal strategy for both players according to the minimax criterion. The situation where both players use this strategy is stable in the sense that when either player realises the other's strategy he has no incentive to change his own. This intuitive analysis affords a clue to the solution of games which do not have saddle points.

Consider the game with the following pay-off matrix:

Player B

		I	II
Player A	I	a	b
	II	c	d

If this game is to have no saddle point the two largest elements of the matrix must constitute one of the diagonals. We assume that this is so and, therefore, both players used mixed strategies. Our task is to determine the probabilities with which both players choose their courses of action. Let player A use his first course of action with probability x and, therefore, his second course of action with probability $(1 - x)$. Let player B's strategy, similarly, be $(y, 1 - y)$. The expected gain resulting from any mixed strategy is a weighted average of the possible outcomes, each outcome being weighted by its probability of occurrence. The expected gain to A if B plays his course of action I throughout is $ax + c(1 - x)$. Similarly, the expected gain to A if B plays his course of action II throughout is $bx + d(1 - x)$. Thus A's expected gain if B plays $(y, 1 - y)$ is

$$y[ax + c(1 - x)] + (1 - y)[bx + d(1 - x)] \tag{1}$$

A's best strategy consists in choosing the value of x such that his guaranteed gain is as large as possible. It can be shown that, in order to achieve this, his expected gain should be the same regardless of B's strategy. This will be so if

$$ax + c(1 - x) = bx + d(1 - x)$$

i.e.

$$x = \frac{d - c}{a + d - (b + c)} \tag{2}$$

A similar argument holds for B, whose best strategy is when

$$y = \frac{d - b}{a + d - (b + c)} \tag{3}$$

The value of the game v is found by substituting the above value of x in one of the expressions for the expected gain of A.

E.g.

$$v = ax + c(1 - x)$$

which on substitution and rearrangement becomes

$$v = \frac{ad - bc}{a + d - (b + c)} \tag{4}$$

The solution of the game is

$$A \text{ plays } (x, 1 - x) \text{ where } x = \frac{d - c}{a + d - (b + c)}$$

$$B \text{ plays } (y, 1 - y) \text{ where } y = \frac{d - b}{a + d - (b + c)}$$

$$v = \frac{ad - bc}{a + d - (b + c)}$$

It should be pointed out that the above analysis assumes that the game has no saddle point. If the game has a saddle point the above result does not hold and the solution of a game with a saddle point is obtained by the simpler method of Example 1.

EXAMPLE 2

Consider a modified form of the game of Matching Pennies, where matching on heads gives a double premium. Obtain the best strategies for both players and the value of the game.

Solution   The pay-off matrix is as follows:

		Player B	
		I (Heads)	II (Tails)
Player A	I (Heads)	2	−1
	II (Tails)	−1	1

Since the largest and second largest elements of the matrix constitute a diagonal, the game has no saddle point, and, hence, the best strategies for both players are mixed strategies. Let player A's strategy be $(x, 1 - x)$ and player B's be $(y, 1 - y)$. Using equations (2), (3) and (4) we obtain,

$$x = \frac{1 - (-1)}{(2 + 1) - (-1 - 1)} = \frac{2}{5}$$

$$y = \frac{1 - (-1)}{5} = \frac{2}{5}$$

$$v = \frac{2 \times 1 - (-1)(-1)}{5} = \frac{1}{5}$$

Both players should play heads $\frac{2}{5}$ of the time. The game is unfair to B as he will lose on average $\frac{1}{5}$ penny per play.

Dominance

We can sometimes reduce the size of a game's pay-off matrix by eliminating a course of action which is so inferior to another as never to be used. Such a course of action is said to be dominated by the other.

EXAMPLE 3

Determine the solution of the game whose pay-off matrix is below:

Player B

$$
\begin{array}{c}
& & \text{I} \quad \text{II} \quad \text{III} \\
& \text{I} & \begin{bmatrix} -4 & 6 & 3 \\ -3 & -3 & 6 \\ 2 & -3 & 4 \end{bmatrix} \\
\textit{Player A} & \text{II} & \\
& \text{III} &
\end{array}
$$

Solution This game has no saddle point. Consider, however, player *B*'s first and third courses of action. From his point of view his first course of action is superior to his third, regardless of *A*'s strategy, the elements in column I being smaller, element for element, than those in column III. Player *B* has no incentive to use his third course of action which is dominated by his first. The effective pay-off matrix is reduced to the one below:

Player B

$$
\begin{array}{c}
& & \text{I} \quad \text{II} \\
& \text{I} & \begin{bmatrix} -4 & 6 \\ -3 & -3 \\ 2 & -3 \end{bmatrix} \\
\textit{Player A} & \text{II} & \\
& \text{III} &
\end{array}
$$

By similar reasoning, player *A*'s third course of action now dominates his second, for although his second and third courses of action are equivalent if *B* chooses II, his third course of action is clearly superior if *B* chooses I. Player *A* has no incentive to choose II and the game reduces to the following:

Player B

$$
\begin{array}{c}
& & \text{I} \quad \text{II} \\
\textit{Player A} & \text{I} & \begin{bmatrix} -4 & 6 \\ 2 & -3 \end{bmatrix} \\
& \text{III} &
\end{array}
$$

This can be solved by the method of the previous example yielding the solution, A plays $(\frac{1}{3}, 0, \frac{2}{3})$, B plays $(\frac{3}{5}, \frac{2}{5}, 0)$ and the value of the game is zero.

'2 × n' games

Games where one player has only two courses of action whilst the other has more than two are called '2 × n' games. It can be shown that, if such games do not have saddle points, there exists, for the player with n courses of action, a combination of just two of these which provides his best strategy. The first part of the solution of such games involves identifying this 2 × 2 sub-game within which lies the solution of the larger game.

EXAMPLE 4
Determine which course of action player B will not use in the following game. Obtain the best strategies for both players and the value of the game.

Player B

$$
\begin{array}{c}
 & \begin{array}{ccc} \text{I} & \text{II} & \text{III} \end{array} \\
\textit{Player A} \quad \begin{array}{c} \text{I} \\ \text{II} \end{array} & \left[\begin{array}{ccc} -3 & -1 & 7 \\ 4 & 1 & -2 \end{array} \right]
\end{array}
$$

Solution   Since there is no saddle point, and since no course of action dominates any other, we consider each 2 × 2 sub-game in turn and find its value. As it is player B who has to make the decision of which courses of action to choose, he will select that pair of courses of action corresponding to the 2 × 2 sub-game the value of which is least.

Considering each 2 × 2 sub-game we obtain the following values:

(*a*)   *Player B*

$$
\begin{array}{c}
 & \begin{array}{cc} \text{I} & \text{II} \end{array} \\
\textit{Player A} \quad \begin{array}{c} \text{I} \\ \text{II} \end{array} & \left[\begin{array}{cc} -3 & -1 \\ 4 & \mathbf{1} \end{array} \right]
\end{array}
$$

This game has a saddle point, shown in bold type above, and its value $v_1 = 1$

(b)

$$\begin{array}{cc} & \textit{Player B} \\ & \text{I} \quad \text{III} \\ \textit{Player A} \quad \begin{array}{c} \text{I} \\ \text{II} \end{array} \left[\begin{array}{cc} -3 & 7 \\ 4 & -2 \end{array} \right] \end{array}$$

The value $v_2 = \dfrac{(-3)(-2) - 7 \times 4}{(-3 - 2) - (7 + 4)} = 1\frac{3}{8}$

(c)

$$\begin{array}{cc} & \textit{Player B} \\ & \text{II} \quad \text{III} \\ \textit{Player A} \quad \begin{array}{c} \text{I} \\ \text{II} \end{array} \left[\begin{array}{cc} -1 & 7 \\ 1 & -2 \end{array} \right] \end{array}$$

The value $v_3 = \dfrac{(-1)(-2) - 7 \times 1}{(-1 - 2) - (7 + 1)} = \dfrac{5}{11}$

The 2×2 sub-game with the lowest value is *(c)* and hence the solution to this game provides the solution to the larger game. Solving *(c)* by the method of Example 2, we find that A chooses I with probability $\frac{3}{11}$, whilst B chooses II with probability $\frac{9}{11}$.

Thus the solution to the larger game is A plays $(\frac{3}{11}, \frac{8}{11})$, B plays $(0, \frac{9}{11}, \frac{2}{11})$, and the value of the game is $\frac{5}{11}$.

The above method of solution is feasible provided that n is small, although it soon becomes laborious as n gets larger. There are three 2×2 sub-games in a 2×3 game, 6 in a 2×4, 10 in a 2×5, etc. An alternative method of solution, useful for larger values of n, is a geometrical method. In order to see the relationship between this method and the former one we shall illustrate its use in relation to Example 4.

Let player A use his first course of action with probability x and his second with probability $(1 - x)$. The expected gain to A if B chooses I throughout is $-3x + 4(1 - x)$, i.e. $4 - 7x$. If we plot a graph of A's gain, g, against the value of x, we see that player B, by choosing I throughout, restricts A's gain to lie on the straight line $g = 4 - 7x$ (see Fig. 8.1).

A's gain if B chooses II throughout is $-x + (1 - x)$, i.e. $1 - 2x$; and A's gain if B chooses III throughout is $7x - 2(1 - x)$, i.e. $9x - 2$.

Plotting these equations $g = 1 - 2x$ and $g = 9x - 2$ we obtain the straight lines which restrict A's gain if B chooses II and III respectively.

Fig. 8.2 overleaf shows the graph with all three lines plotted.

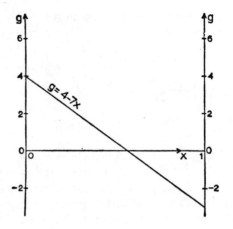

Fig. 8.1   Graph of $g = 4 - 7x$

If we bound the series of lines so formed from below, points on the lines *PQ RS* represent the lowest possible expected gains to *A* for any value of *x* between 0 and 1.

According to the minimax criterion, *A* chooses the best of these worst outcomes. This is represented by point *Q*. Reading from the graph the values of *x* and *g* at this point, $x = \frac{3}{11}$ and $g = \frac{5}{11}$. It can also be deduced from the graph that *B* should not employ his first

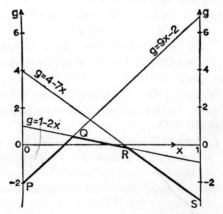

Fig. 8.2   Graphical solution of '2 × *n*' game

course of action, as this does not confine A's gain to $\frac{5}{11}$. Thus the 2 × 2 sub-game within which lies the solution to the 2 × 3 game is:

Player B

$$\begin{array}{cc} & \begin{array}{cc} \text{II} & \text{III} \end{array} \\ \textit{Player A} \quad \begin{array}{c} \text{I} \\ \text{II} \end{array} & \left[\begin{array}{cc} -1 & 7 \\ 1 & -2 \end{array} \right] \end{array}$$

from which B's best strategy may be determined.

Both of the above methods apply equally well if it is player A who has more than two courses of action. In this case, in the first method A selects his two courses of action corresponding to the 2 × 2 sub-game whose value is greatest. In the second method, the graph plotted is A's gain against the value of y (the probability with which B uses his first course of action). The series of lines so formed is bounded from above, and the solution lies in player B choosing the value of y which corresponds to the lowest point on this boundary.

Exploiting an opponent's mistakes

We have so far considered the best strategies for both players in a two-person game. The definition of 'best strategy' implies that the game is being played against a rational opponent whose object is to maximise his own gain. It is possible for player A to take advantage of the knowledge that player B is not using his best strategy.

Consider further the game on page 163. Player A's strategy of $(\frac{1}{2}, \frac{1}{2})$ is optimal against a shrewd opponent in that it protects him against loss. If, however, B is observed to play 'heads' more frequently than 'tails', A can increase his gain by also playing 'heads' more frequently than 'tails'. If, for example, B plays 'heads' twice as often as 'tails', i.e. a strategy of $(\frac{2}{3}, \frac{1}{3})$, A increases his gain by also choosing for his strategy $(\frac{2}{3}, \frac{1}{3})$. The gain to A under these circumstances is $\frac{2}{3}(\frac{1}{3}) + \frac{1}{3}(-\frac{1}{3})$, i.e. $\frac{1}{9}$, player A winning, on average, 5 games out of 9. It can be shown that if the opponent's strategy is known in advance, a player achieves his maximum gain by employing a pure strategy. Thus in this example, A could increase his gain to $\frac{1}{3}$ by playing heads throughout. Unfortunately, if A did this, B would almost certainly notice and be led to modify his own strategy. The problem for A in practice is to exploit B's blunders without showing him the error of his ways.

In the foregoing discussion, the concept of a mixed strategy implies that a game is to be played a number of times. What of games that are played only once? It is true that the implication has been that games are repeatable. The reason for this is that in a mixed strategy it is intuitively easier to imagine the probabilities of the various choices as the frequencies with which each course of action would be chosen if the game were repeated many times. The meaning of the term 'expected gain' is also more readily understood under this assumption. In fact, the results hold whether a game is to be played only once or repeated many times. Indeed, the more strategic the decision, in terms of the importance of its conse- quence, the more likely it is to be a 'one-off' decision and not part of a series. In such a case, if the analysis suggests a mixed strategy, it is of paramount importance that no hint of the proposed action be given in advance. By using a chance device the decision-maker ensures that he chooses a course of action that his opponent cannot anticipate. The probabilities given by his mixed strategy determine the characteristics of the chance device he should use.

EXAMPLE 5

A has two ammunition stores, one of which is twice as valuable as the other. B is an attacker who can destroy an undefended store but he can only attack one of them. A can successfully defend only one of them. A learns that B is about to attack one of the stores but does not know which. What should he do?

Solution   The value of the smaller store is 1, the value of the larger store is 2.

If both stores survive, A loses nothing.

If only the larger survives, A loses 1.

If only the smaller survives, A loses 2.

Since both parties have only two possible courses of action, A's pay-off matrix is as follows:

$$
\begin{array}{c}
 & & B \\
 & & \begin{array}{cc} \textit{Attack} & \textit{Attack} \\ \textit{smaller store} & \textit{larger store} \end{array} \\
A \quad \begin{array}{c} \textit{Defend} \\ \textit{smaller store} \\ \textit{Defend} \\ \textit{larger store} \end{array} & \left[\begin{array}{cc} 0 & -2 \\ \\ -1 & 0 \end{array} \right]
\end{array}
$$

Before analysing this problem as a game, let us consider how A and B might otherwise reason in the real situation. A would argue that he cannot afford to take the risk of losing the larger ammunition store and therefore he must defend this one. If B is shrewd, however, he would anticipate A's reasoning and attack the smaller store with a certain gain of 1. Thus A's 'logic' would result in a gain of -1.

The problem may be solved by the methods outlined earlier. A's best strategy is the mixed strategy $(\frac{1}{3}, \frac{2}{3})$ and the value of the game is $-\frac{2}{3}$. In order to make his decision, therefore, A should roll a die. He should defend the smaller store if a 1 or 2 turns up; otherwise he should defend the larger one. This strategy leads to a more favourable expected outcome than the 'logic' mentioned above.

Having illustrated how a 'one-off' decision should be reached, we know that decisions in practice are not made in the above manner. An executive would probably not inspire confidence in his ability if it were known that he made his decisions by selecting a number at random; and what manager would ascribe to the toss of a coin the credit for a decision which proved successful – or catastrophic? There is an important difference between games and many of the decisions that have to be made in practice.

By definition, in a game nothing is known of an opponent's strategy, save that he is an extremely shrewd player. In many decision-making situations, however, this is not so, and even where there is an opponent the decision is often based on some knowledge of his likely strategy.

Games against Nature

We have shown in the previous section how a player may take advantage of knowledge of his opponent's strategy. Many decision-making situations can be viewed as zero-sum two-person games where the opponent is Nature. Such a situation differs from a game in that Nature is not actively engaged in trying to outwit her opponent. Her behaviour is independent of her opponent's and may well be to some extent predictable. This being so, a player against Nature should be able to select that pure strategy which maximises his expected gain.

EXAMPLE 6

On a warm summer day we decide to take a walk. Should we take a mac?

Solution   In order to formulate this problem we need to know two facts:

(a) The probability of rain.
(b) The relative inconvenience of carrying a mac in warm weather compared with that of being caught in the rain without one.

Suppose we look at the sky and judge that the probability of rain is $\frac{1}{10}$. Further suppose that we rate it four times as inconvenient being caught in the rain without a mac as having to carry a mac in warm weather. The situation is represented below:

$$
\begin{array}{c}
 & & \text{Nature} \\
 & & \text{Rain} \quad \text{No rain} \\
\text{Take mac} & & \begin{bmatrix} 0 & -1 \\ & \\ -4 & 0 \end{bmatrix} \\
\text{Decision-maker} & & \\
\text{Go without mac} & &
\end{array}
$$

(It could be that we may also judge it inconvenient to be caught in the rain even whilst wearing a mac. However, the problem is not whether or not we should take a walk – this has been decided already on other grounds.) Assessing each of our courses of action in turn we obtain:

Expected gain if mac is taken is $-\frac{9}{10}$.
Expected gain if mac is not taken is $-\frac{4}{10}$.

Carrying a mac, therefore, constitutes more inconvenience than not carrying one. This remains the case as long as the probability of rain is less than $\frac{1}{5}$.

In everyday life we are constantly making decisions; some trivial, as in the previous example, some not so trivial. Although we rarely, if ever, formulate the decision in detail, as above, we may nevertheless unconsciously carry out a similar exercise. There are decisions, however, where the issues are of such importance as to demand time for quantitative analysis. It is in such situations that game theory is valuable. Its ultimate usefulness in practice depends on how exhaustively the courses of action may be determined and how accurately the possible outcomes may be measured. Game theory does at least provide a framework within which the relevant factors involved in a decision may be isolated.

Before leaving the subject of game theory we give an interesting example of a non zero-sum game known as 'The prisoners' dilemma'. Two prisoners are being held for questioning in connection with a serious crime. The superintendent of police is convinced that both men are guilty but has insufficient evidence to convict them. He decides to interrogate the prisoners separately and warns that if one confesses and the other refuses to confess, the penalty will be particularly servere for the one who denies the charge, whilst the one who confesses will go free for giving testimony against the other. Both prisoners know that if neither confesses they will both receive at most a minor sentence for a technical offence. Each prisoner's pay-off matrix, in terms of prison sentences, may be represented as follows:

	Accomplice denies	*Accomplice confesses*
Deny the charge	$\begin{bmatrix} 3 \text{ months} \\ \text{Go free} \end{bmatrix}$	$\begin{matrix} 10 \text{ years} \\ 6 \text{ years} \end{matrix}$
Confess		

Assuming both prisoners behave rationally and have no qualms about testifying against their accomplice – there being no honour among thieves – they will both decide to confess, this course of action dominating the other. The result is that both prisoners receive a 6-year sentence compared with the 3-month sentence if neither confessed. It is unlikely that the overall optimum solution for the prisoners – both denying the charge – can be reached without collusion. This situation is similar to that which obtains when rival marketing organisations consider the effects of price cutting. That the similarity is appreciated is demonstrated by the existence of agreements between companies not to sell below a fixed price.

Exercises

Solve the following zero-sum two-person games. Obtain the best strategies for both players and the value of the game:

8.1

Player B

$$
\begin{array}{c}
 & \begin{array}{cc} \text{I} & \text{II} \end{array} \\
Player A \quad \begin{array}{c} \text{I} \\ \text{II} \end{array} & \left[\begin{array}{cc} 1 & 1 \\ 0 & 2 \end{array} \right]
\end{array}
$$

8.2

Player B

$$
\begin{array}{cc}
 & \begin{array}{ccccc} \text{I} & \text{II} & \text{III} & \text{IV} & \text{V} \end{array} \\
Player A \begin{array}{c} \text{I} \\ \text{II} \\ \text{III} \\ \text{IV} \\ \text{V} \end{array} & \left[\begin{array}{ccccc} 4 & 0 & 1 & 7 & -1 \\ 0 & -3 & -5 & -7 & 5 \\ 3 & 2 & 3 & 4 & 3 \\ -6 & 1 & -1 & 0 & 5 \\ 0 & 0 & 6 & 0 & 0 \end{array} \right]
\end{array}
$$

8.3

Player B

$$
\begin{array}{cc}
 & \begin{array}{ccc} \text{I} & \text{II} & \text{III} \end{array} \\
Player A \begin{array}{c} \text{I} \\ \text{II} \\ \text{III} \\ \text{IV} \end{array} & \left[\begin{array}{ccc} 1 & -1 & 3 \\ 2 & -1 & 2 \\ -1 & 0 & 0 \\ -2 & 0 & 4 \end{array} \right]
\end{array}
$$

8.4

Player B

$$
\begin{array}{cc}
 & \begin{array}{ccc} \text{I} & \text{II} & \text{III} \end{array} \\
Player A \begin{array}{c} \text{I} \\ \text{II} \\ \text{III} \end{array} & \left[\begin{array}{ccc} -5 & 1 & -1 \\ 4 & 0 & 2 \\ -5 & 2 & 0 \end{array} \right]
\end{array}
$$

8.5 You are invited to play a modified version of 'Matching Pennies'. The matching player is paid £8 if the two coins are both heads and £1 if the coins are both tails. The non-matching player is paid £3 when the coins do not match. Given the choice of being the matching player or the non-matching player which would you choose, and what would be your strategy?

8.6 What is the best strategy for player *A* in the following game?

$$
\begin{array}{cc}
 & \textit{Player B} \\
 & \begin{array}{cc} \text{I} & \text{II} \end{array}
\end{array}
$$

$$
\textit{Player A}
\begin{array}{c}
\text{I} \\ \text{II} \\ \text{III} \\ \text{IV} \\ \text{V}
\end{array}
\left[
\begin{array}{rr}
3 & -5 \\
1 & -1 \\
2 & -3 \\
-1 & 3 \\
0 & 1
\end{array}
\right]
$$

8.7 Suppose you were playing the following word-game. You are required to select two of the consonants K, N and R, and your opponent one of the vowels A or I. If the three letters chosen make up words your opponent pays you £1 for each word which starts with a vowel and £2 for each word which starts with a consonant. If the letters do not form a word you pay your opponent £3.

  (*a*) What strategy would you adopt and what would be your expected gain?

  (*b*) Is there any strategy that your opponent could use which would make you decide to change your own?

9

Network Analysis

Introduction

Network analysis embraces a set of logical and mathematical models which can be represented graphically in the form of a network. Such a representation is familiar for systems of electrical circuits and transport route structures. It is perhaps less familiar in the context of accountancy and the preparations for building, manning and launching a rocket to the moon. The form that analysis takes depends on the objective to be achieved and on special characteristics of the network. Before discussing applications it is necessary to define a few of the concepts that arise with networks.

Networks

A *network* or *linear graph* consists of a number of points or *nodes*, each of which is connected to one or more of the other nodes by *routes* or *edges*. Thus Fig. 9.1 opposite illustrates a network with nodes and 9 edges.

Two nodes are *adjacent* if there is an edge connecting them. Two edges are adjacent if there is a node common to both. A *chain* is a sequence of adjacent edges. A *cycle* is a finite chain which begins and ends at the same node. A *loop* is an edge connecting a node to itself. Examples of these are also shown in Fig. 9.1.

In many networks the sequencing or ordering of two nodes is of significance. Therefore an *arc* is a *directed* edge. An (undirected) edge can always be represented by two arcs, one from the first to the

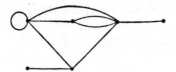

Fig. 9.1   A network

second node and one from the second to the first node. Thus there is no loss of generality in discussing a network in terms of arcs and nodes.

A *path* is a sequence of arcs in a network, such that the terminal node of each arc (except the last) coincides with the initial node of the succeeding arc. If the network has a node to which it is impossible to return, this initial node is a *source*. If there is a node from which it is impossible to return, this terminal node is a *sink*. A *circuit* is a finite path in which the initial node and final node coincide.

EXAMPLE 1
The network in Fig. 9.2 below is one derived by directing each edge and numbering each node in Fig. 9.1. List the properties of this network.

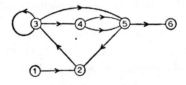

Fig. 9.2   A directed network

Solution   Some of the properties of this network are:

(*a*) there is at least one path from node 1 to all other nodes;
(*b*) node 1 is the only source;
(*c*) node 6 is the only sink;
(*d*) the arcs (1, 2), (5, 2), (5, 6) are a chain but not a path;
(*e*) there are two arcs, from node 4 to node 5, which form a cycle but not a circuit;

(*f*) there are three circuits, through nodes 2, 3 and 5 and nodes 2, 3, 4 and 5;

(*g*) there is one loop, at node 3.

Critical path scheduling

The context

Critical path scheduling is a group of network analysis techniques which have been applied to the planning and control of such operations as:

Construction: buildings, bridges, chemical plant
Maintenance: annual shut-down of heavy plant
Retooling: modifying a machine in a production process
Launching: a new product, a missile
Research and development: US Polaris programme
Accountancy: budgeting and auditing procedures
Mobilisation: strategic and tactical planning

These operations have the following common characteristics:

Activities: the operation can be analysed into many separate activities, each taking time.
Logic: the nature of the operation is such that some activities must precede others and some activities are carried out in parallel with others.
Resources: each activity requires some combination of resources of men, machines, materials, or money. Usually there is more than one possible combination of resources for any activity.

The network

These operations can be represented by a network in which an arc represents an activity and a node represents an event (the start or

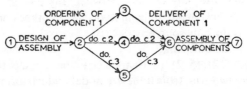

Fig. 9.3 The network of an assembly operation

finish of one or more activities). The structure of the network then represents the logical sequencing of the different activities. Thus Fig. 9.3 shows a network representation of the operation of designing an assembly, ordering and delivery of the three components, and assembling them.

If the duration of each activity, as well as their logical sequence, is known, it can be indicated on a network as in Fig. 9.4. The duration might be measured in days in this example.

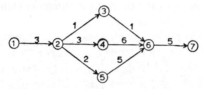

Fig. 9.4   Activity durations on the network

It is common practice to number the nodes so that all subsequent nodes have higher numbers than their predecessors, though they need not be consecutive as in Fig. 9.4. This enables certain checks to be made quite simply during analysis, but it restricts the number of additional arcs and nodes that can be added to the network if this should become necessary. When flexibility of this kind is of great importance, a system of numbering nodes at random can be used at the expense of more cumbersome checking procedures. In either type of system an arc is referred to by the number of its initial and terminal node.

Characteristics of the network
The network used in critical path scheduling has the following special properties:

1 Conventionally there is one and only one initial node and one terminal node of the whole network.
2 There is one and only one arc between any pair of connected nodes. (It is always possible to add *dummy* nodes and arcs to create this property if it does not exist already.)
3 There are no circuits.
4 There are no loops.
5 There is at least one path from the initial node to all succeeding nodes, and in particular to the terminal node.

6 If each activity has a known duration, and assuming that all the necessary resources are available, each path from the initial node to the terminal node can be assigned a duration (the sum of the individual activity times involved).

7 The duration of the whole operation is that of the longest path. Any delay to the activities on this path increases the duration of the whole operation, whereas any (suitably small) delay to activities not on this path does not. Such a longest path is called a *critical path* and the activities on it *critical activities*. There may well be more than one critical path.

In Fig. 9.4 the nodes 1, 2, 4, 6 and 7 define the critical activities, the critical path length is 17 days and there are non-critical paths of length 15 days and 10 days. Thus, if the estimates of duration are correct, only component 2 is affecting the duration of the whole operation.

8 The difference in time between the earliest that a non-critical activity can be completed and the time that it must be completed to avoid becoming critical itself is the *activity float* or *slack*. An activity that can be delayed by its activity float without interfering with other activities has *free float*. An activity that can only be delayed by its activity float at the expense of some adjacent activity's float has *interfering float*.

In Fig. 9.4 there is no free float, but activities (2, 3) and (3, 6) have interfering float of 7 days, and activities (2, 5) and (5, 6) have interfering float of 2 days.

9 It may be convenient to group all those activities with small positive float as *sub-critical* activities, since only small changes in duration could make them critical.

In a network as small as that in Fig. 9.4 this is hardly appropriate, but for very large networks a list of sub-critical activities is useful management information.

Objective

Critical path scheduling may be used to plan an operation, in order to achieve any one of the following objectives:

1 **Minimise total time** It may be technologically essential to carry out a complex operation in the shortest possible time, regardless of cost. It may also be, for example, that the cost of lost

production, while a maintenance operation is carried out, is so high that it is economically justifiable to spend on resources whatever is necessary in order to minimise the time of the operation.

2 **Minimise total cost** When the cost of delay in the completion of the operation can be measured, as well as the cost of the resources required to carry out the operation at various speeds, it is possible to take both types of cost into account and to minimise the total cost of the whole operation.

3 **Minimise cost for a given total time** When the operation is to take a given total time, it may be desirable to arrange resources for the operation so that this time is achieved at minimum cost.

4 **Minimise time for a given cost** When a fixed sum is available, it may be desirable to arrange resources for the operation so that the total time is minimised without the sum allowed being exceeded.

5 **Minimise idle resources** It may be desirable to avoid having wide variations in the use of resources, e.g. labour, during an operation. This would normally increase the duration of the operation relative to a plan allowing more variable resource utilisation.

Versions of critical path scheduling
There are many versions of critical path scheduling procedures with greater or less degrees of sophistication and flexibility. Those mentioned below are the two most well known:

CPM (Critical Path Method) The duration of every activity is assumed to be constant and known (see Fig. 9.4 for example). Therefore every activity is either critical or not.

PERT (Program Evaluation and Review Technique) Uncertainty in the duration of activities is allowed and is measured by three parameters:

Most optimistic duration (lower bound)
Most likely duration (greatest frequency or mode)
Most pessimistic duration (upper bound).

Since in most situations activities can be delayed much more than they can be accelerated, the most pessimistic estimate is very much further from the most likely duration than the most optimistic duration is. Therefore the average duration of an activity is longer than its most likely duration. Assuming a particular type of frequency distribution of the time of an activity, the mean time of each activity is calculated. Assuming that they are all independent, the mean time of each path is the sum of the mean times of the relevant activities. Then the greatest of these is taken as the estimate of the average duration of the whole project.

With the uncertainty attached to the duration of each activity, it is not possible to divide all activities into those which are critical and those which are not. Activities can only be sorted according to the degree of probability that they will be critical. Uncertainty in the data, however, and doubts about the validity of the further assumptions made, may prevent this refinement being worthwhile.

Analysis

A critical path schedule provides details of the timing of activities and their resource requirements throughout the duration of the whole operation. It directs attention to the critical activities, which are not necessarily the larger jobs or the later jobs. Management by exception can easily be implemented by listing only critical and near critical activities. During a project, progress information is used to update the schedule and produce a revised analysis. This provides a useful means of dealing with unexpected developments, especially when these involve a main contractor and subcontractors. Indeed it is becoming increasingly the practice that tenders for a contract have to be submitted on the basis of critical path scheduling.

There are standard computer programs for various forms of critical path scheduling. Once the basic information has been compiled, it is easy to produce analyses not only of critical activities, but also of all activities by a given trade and the scheduled dates for these.

Linear programming – transportation

The transportation method of linear programming can be carried out in the form of a network problem as an alternative to operating on a series of tables.

EXAMPLE 2

Example 2 in Chapter 7 concerned the distribution of items from four warehouses to three customers. Reformulate this problem in terms of a network.

Solution A minimum cost allocation was given in Table 7.8, which is produced here as Fig. 9.5:

Warehouses

		a	*b*	*c*	*d*	
	Shadow costs	4	9	3	3	*Required*
A	0	(4) 8	4 9	(3) 6	13 3	17
B	2	9 6	(0) 11	11 5	(5) 10	20
C	−1	6 3	12 8	(5) 7	(7) 9	18
	Available	15	16	11	13	55

Customers (label for the left row group)

Fig. 9.5 Second iteration of Example 2, Chapter 7

The four warehouses and three customers can be represented by seven points, and, since each customer could be supplied from any warehouse, the network of all twelve possible routes would be:

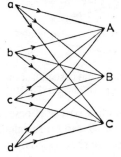

Fig. 9.6 All possible routes (4, 3) transportation problem

The particular selection of routes given in Fig. 9.5 is then represented by Fig. 9.7:

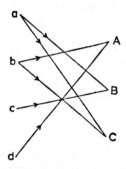

Fig. 9.7 A minimum cost selection of routes

By rearranging the order of the warehouses and of the customers, this network can be presented more clearly, together with the items available, the items allocated to each route, and the items required, in Fig. 9.8:

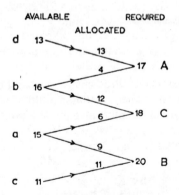

Fig. 9.8 A minimum cost allocation of used routes

As in Chapter 7, the shadow cost of A is set arbitrarily at 0 and the shadow costs of a, b, c, d, B and C are calculated to be 4, 9, 3, 3, 2 and -1 respectively. These shadow costs are shown in brackets in Fig. 9.9:

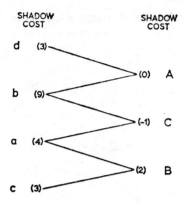

Fig. 9.9 Shadow costs for minimum cost allocation

The sum of the two shadow costs on each of the routes being *used* is equal to the unit transportation cost on that route, given in Table 7.1. This part of the calculation depends on there being one and only one chain between each node and every other node, and a network having this property is a *tree*. Having calculated the shadow costs, the *unused* routes have to be tested. Fig. 9.10 is the network of unused routes, derived by selecting all those routes in Fig. 9.6 not in Fig. 9.7 and with the warehouses and customers arranged in the original order. Each unused route is labelled with its unit transportation cost, and each warehouse and customer is labelled with its shadow cost. As in Chapter 7, the difference between transportation cost and the sum of the shadow costs is not negative for any of the unused routes, as is quickly seen from Fig. 9.10. Therefore no unused route would give a reduction in total cost if it was used, and hence the allocation of used routes in Fig. 9.8 is a minimum cost solution. If, at some earlier stage in the calculation, an unused route had a negative difference, then it would have been profitable to introduce that route into the network of used routes, and to remove a used route into the network of unused routes. In so doing, the allocations, the shadow costs, and the network of unused routes would all be modified. The process would be repeated until no unused route had a negative difference. Then a minimum cost solution would have been found.

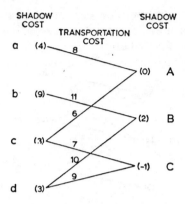

Fig. 9.10   Routes not used in minimum cost allocation

The transportation problem can be restated, therefore, in the following network terms:

Given *m* source nodes and *n* sink nodes, and the cost of sending a unit from every source to every sink, the network consists of $m + n$ nodes and *mn* arcs. Find a set of $(m + n - 1)$ of these arcs in the form of a tree, such that:

   (i) specified numbers of units required arrive at the sink nodes from
  (ii) specified numbers of units available at the source nodes
 (iii) at minimum total cost.

In a degenerative problem it is possible to do this with less than $(m + n - 1)$ arcs. Thus the solution ceases to be a single tree but becomes two or more trees, i.e. a *forest*. The assignment problem is the most degenerate case, in which there are only $m = n$ used routes and the solution is a forest of *m* single-arc trees.

Further network problems

Network flow
The transportation problem is to find the cheapest flow from sources to sinks, with given costs per unit flow on each arc and with unlimited arc capacities. In a different context a network may have

each arc with a maximum flow capacity, and the problem is to determine the maximum possible flow through the network.

The network in Fig. 9.11 has a single source and a single sink. Each arc has the maximum capacity shown.

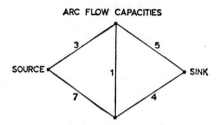

Fig. 9.11 Flow through a network with limited capacities

Consider the problem in terms not of a maximal flow but of a minimal cut. A cut is a set of arcs that it would be necessary to blow up in order to prevent any flow reaching the sink. The value of such a cut is the sum of the arc capacities concerned. The smallest of these values is the value of the minimal cut. As Ford and Fulkerson prove in their book *Flows in Networks*, the maximal flow is equal to the minimal cut. If the maximal flow was greater than the minimal cut, then blowing up the minimal cut would not stop all flow and hence the minimal cut would not be a cut. This is a contradiction, and therefore the maximal flow cannot be greater than the minimal cut. A flow can be less than the minimal cut, but if it is, it is clearly not maximal. Therefore the maximal flow equals the minimal cut.

EXAMPLE 3

Determine the maximal flow through the network in Fig. 9.11.

Solution There are four cuts, of which the values are:

$$
\begin{array}{llll}
3 & & +7 & & = 10 \\
& 5 & & +4 & = 9 \\
3 & +1 & & +4 & = 8 \\
& 5 & +1 & +7 & = 13
\end{array}
$$

The minimal cut is, therefore, 8. The maximal flow is obtained by saturating the arcs concerned, with other arcs flowing at less than full capacity. In this example there is only one way of getting maximal flow, and this is shown in Fig. 9.12.

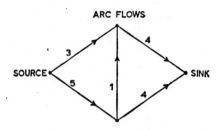

Fig. 9.12 Maximal flow through the network

Replacement

Use of a network, in the form of a failure tree, was illustrated in Chapter 3 in keeping track of different categories of items that failed and had to be replaced. A failure tree always has a source, indicating the initial situation with completely new items. At each node except the source there is one incoming arc. At each node that is not a sink there are usually two out-going arcs but sometimes only one. It is impossible for a failure tree to degenerate into a forest, and two branches can never come together.

Dynamic programming

Multi-stage decision processes can in some cases be formulated as finding the shortest or longest path through a network with many connections. A procedure for carrying out the calculation is illustrated in the next chapter.

Exercises

9.1 Construct a network for a project (such as an annual maintenance) which consists of the following activities:

Activity		Activity time	Resources
Initial node	*Terminal node*	*(days)*	*(no. of men)*
0	1	1	1
1	2	2	1
1	4	3	1
2	3	4	1
3	4	16	2
3	5	14	1
3	6	14	2
4	7	12	2
4	8	14	3
4	9	10	1
5	10	0	0
6	10	0	0
7	10	5	1
8	10	4	2
9	10	6	1
10	11	3	2

Calculate the critical path(s) and the total duration of the project.

9.2 How many paths (of all kinds) are there?

9.3 On the same network show the activity floats, distinguishing between free float and interfering. Hence list sub-critical activities, e.g. with float not more than 7 days.

9.4 How many men are actually required on each day of the project, given that there are six available?

9.5 Is the critical path altered if there are only five men available. If so, what are the new critical events, what is the new project duration and what are the new floats?

10

Dynamic Programming

Introduction

One method of deciding how best to allocate resources, linear programming, was described in Chapter 7. There are, however, other methods which are relevant to similar problems, but which do not demand some of the assumptions needed for linear programming. One such method is dynamic programming. Programming is used in the mathematical sense of selecting an optimum allocation of resources, and it is dynamic in the sense that it is particularly useful for problems where decisions are taken at several distinct stages, such as every day or every week.

A traveller and the principle of optimality

EXAMPLE 1

A traveller at A wishes to reach his destination H by the shortest route. Suppose that the alternative routes and the inter-city distances (not to scale) are as shown in Fig. 10.1 opposite.

By looking at all the possible routes, it is clear that the shortest lies through B and E, giving a total distance of $3 + 2 + 1 = 6$. The four other routes are $ACEH$ (7), $ACFH$ (9), $ACGH$ (10) and $ADGH$ (11). If the traveller wants only to go as far as E, one of the intermediate cities on his shortest route from A to H, which route should he choose? Of the two possible routes, the one to E through C is longer (6) than the one through B (5), so he chooses the route ABE. This is exactly the same route taken as when he is going all the

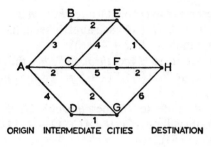

Fig. 10.1 A routing problem

way on to H by the shortest route. Indeed the route $ABEH$ would not be the shortest if it were better to reach E through C than through B. Since the traveller is considering stopping at intermediate cities only on the overall shortest route, we can state the following principle:

The principle of optimality The overall shortest route from origin to destination contains the shortest route from the origin to any of the intermediate cities on the overall shortest route

or

the overall shortest route from origin to destination contains the shortest route from any of the intermediate cities on the overall shortest route to the destination.

If you do not yet think that these two equivalent statements are obvious, change the distances given in Fig. 10.1 and recalculate the shortest route, both to the destination and to all the intermediate cities.

The principle involved in these statements of a property of the shortest route through the network can be illustrated further as follows. Suppose that the distances from E, F and G to H are as yet unknown. Then we cannot tell which of the five possible routes is the shortest, but we can still make the following conditional statements:

If the distances EH, FH and GH turn out to be such that:

1. the shortest route to *H* goes *through E, then* the overall shortest route will be *ABEH*; (we have already seen that *ABE* (3 + 2 = 5) is shorter than *ACE* (2 + 4 = 6));
2. the shortest route to *H* goes *through F, then* the overall shortest route will be *ACFH*; (*ACF* (2 + 5 = 7) is the only possibility in this case);
2. the shortest route to *H* goes *through G, then* the overall shortest route will be *ACGH*; (*ACG* (2 + 2 = 4) is shorter than *ADG* (4 + 1 = 5)).

Therefore, the length of the overall shortest route will be either:

	shortest route to *E* (5) + *EH*
or	shortest route to *F* (7) + *FH*
or	shortest route to *G* (4) + *GH*

whichever is the smallest of the three. As soon as the distances *EG*, *FH* and *GH* become known, we can carry out this comparison and hence determine the shortest route from *A* to *H*.

In considering this shortest route problem, we have assumed that the total distance is the sum of the distances between the relevant cities, and that each inter-city distance is known in advance and is fixed. This simple property might not apply if some variable other than distance is being minimised.

A more complex routing problem

EXAMPLE 2
The network in Example 1 is so small that the principle stated hardly seems significant. Consider the more complex network shown in Fig. 10.2, with three intermediate stages and three possible choices of route at all but the last cities.

This figure is clearly not drawn to scale; indeed, suppose that the numbers by each inter-city connection represent a variable such as the *time* taken to travel between the two cities. Which intermediate cities are visited if the time taken to get from *P* to *Z* is to be as small as possible?

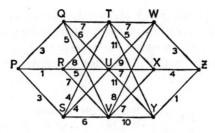

Fig. 10.2 A more complex routing problem

Solution Starting from P, consider the problem in stages:

First: Q, R or S?
Second: T, U or V?
Third: W, X or Y?
Final: Best route to Z?

First stage: We do not know yet whether the quickest route lies through Q, but *if it does* the quickest route from P to Q is obviously PQ. Similar statements about getting to R and to S are equally obvious. Thus:

$$\left.\begin{array}{l} P \text{ to } Q = 3 \\ P \text{ to } R = 1 \\ P \text{ to } S = 3 \end{array}\right\} \begin{array}{l} \text{by the shortest and} \\ \text{only route} \end{array}$$

Second stage: We do not know yet whether the quickest route lies through T, but *if it does*, would it have gone through Q, R or S? Now the route PQT takes $3 + 7 = 10$, PRT takes $1 + 8 = 9$ and PST takes $3 + 4 = 7$. Therefore the quickest way to T is through S, though we still may not go through T at all, once we know the overall quickest route.

We do not know yet whether the quickest route lies through U rather than T. But *if it does*, would it have gone through Q, R or S? Now the route PQU takes $3 + 6 = 9$, PRU takes $1 + 5 = 6$ and PSU takes $3 + 4 = 7$. Therefore the quickest way to U is through R, though we still may not go through U at all, once we know the overall quickest route.

To finish the second stage, we do not know yet whether the quickest route lies through V rather than T or U. But *if it does*, would it have gone through Q, R or S? Now the route PQV takes $3 + 5 = 8$, PRV takes $1 + 7 = 8$ also, and PSV takes $3 + 6 = 9$. Therefore the quickest way to V is through either Q or R, though we still may not go through V at all, once we know the overall quickest route. Thus:

$$\left.\begin{array}{l} P \text{ to } T = 7 \\ P \text{ to } U = 6 \\ P \text{ to } V = 8 \end{array}\right\} \text{ by the quickest route}$$

Third stage: We do not know yet whether the quickest route lies through W, but *if it does*, would it have gone through T, U or V? Now the route PTW takes $7 + 7 = 14$ if T is reached by the quickest route; PUW takes $6 + 9 = 15$ if U is reached by the quickest route; PVW takes $8 + 8 = 16$ if V is reached by the quickest route. Therefore the quickest way to W is through T, provided that T itself was reached in the quickest way (through S). We still may not go through W, T or S at all, once we know the overall quickest route.

We do not know yet whether the best route lies through X rather than W. But *if it does*, would it have gone through T, U or V? Now the route PTX takes $7 + 5 = 12$ if T is reached by the quickest route; PUX takes $6 + 7 = 13$ if U is reached by the quickest route; PVX takes $8 + 7 = 15$ if V is reached by the quickest route. Therefore the quickest way to X is through T, provided that T itself was reached in the quickest way (through S). We still may not go through X, T or S at all, once we know the overall quickest route.

To finish the third stage, we do not know yet whether the best route lies through Y rather than W or X. But *if it does*, would it have gone through T, U or V? Now the route PTY takes $7 + 11 = 18$ if T is reached by the quickest route; PUY takes $6 + 11 = 17$ if U is reached by the quickest route; PVY takes $8 + 10 = 18$ if V is reached by the quickest route. Therefore the quickest way to Y is through U, provided that U itself was reached in the quickest way (through R). We still may not go through Y, U or R at all, once we know the overall quickest route. Thus:

$$\left.\begin{array}{l} P \text{ to } W = 14 \\ P \text{ to } X = 12 \\ P \text{ to } Y = 17 \end{array}\right\} \text{ by the quickest route}$$

Final stage: We can now calculate the quickest route from P to Z. P to W by the quickest route and on to Z takes $14 + 3 = 17$; P to X by the quickest route and on to Z takes $12 + 4 = 16$; P to Y by the quickest route and on to Z takes $17 + 1 = 18$. Therefore the quickest route from P to Z takes 16.

We can trace our steps back through the network and determine which intermediate cities lie on the quickest route from P to Z. We know from the final stage of the calculation that X does. This implies (from the third stage) that T also does, since the quickest route from P to X is through T. This in turn implies (from the second stage) that S also is on the quickest route from P to Z, since the quickest route from P to T is through S.

The quickest route, therefore, runs from P through S, T and X to Z, taking a total time of 16. This is also the quickest route from Z to P, since in this problem none of the times depend on the direction of travel. Example 2 has been solved with sub-routes from P, i.e. forwards. Once Z was reached, the quickest route was specified by retracing our steps through the relevant sub-routes. But we could have solved the problem by starting from Z, i.e. backwards, and looking at sub-routes to Z until P was reached. This procedure would have reached the same quickest route between P and Z, but would have involved a different sequence of sub-problems.

Even though we shall actually be travelling from P to Z, there are advantages in using the backwards approach, i.e. knowing the quickest sub-route from any city to Z. In this way, had we taken a wrong turning to a city not on the overall quickest route, we would still know how to go from that city to Z in the quickest way. The result of our mistake is a longer journey, of course, but at least we can make an optimal recovery from our mistake. Why pay more for this than we have to?

The backwards solution to Example 2 is set as an exercise for the reader at the end of the chapter. In some cases only a backwards solution may be possible, and such a case is illustrated by Example 3.

A problem involving probability

In the previous examples it was convenient, but not essential, to describe the problems in terms of a network. This represented a number of intermediate stages at which alternative decisions forward were possible. By using the principle of optimality a sequence of sub-problems was solved until the overall shortest route was determined. In both cases only one quantity (either distance or time) was attached to an inter-city route, and it was assumed that all such quantities were constant and known. Dynamic programming can also be used to optimise multi-stage decision processes involving probability, as illustrated by the next example.

EXAMPLE 3
Consider the following five-stage network:

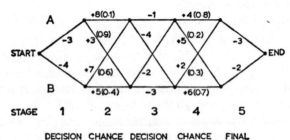

Fig. 10.3   A five-stage probabilistic problem

This network could represent some kind of system that can be in one of the two states, say A or B, at any time. The sequence of changes through the five stages is as follows.

Stage 1: Initially the system can be put either into state A at a cost of 3 or into state B at a cost of 4. (A cost has a negative sign in the diagram.)

Stage 2: Then chance factors operate, so that either the system remains in the same state or it changes to the other state, with the known probabilities given in brackets. There is also a return associated with each possibility. (A return has a positive sign in the diagram.) Thus if the system is in state A, the chance that it will remain in state A is 0·1 and the return will be +8 if it does.

Stage 3: Once the outcome of this uncertainty is known, the system can again either be maintained in its present state or be changed to the other state, both at a given cost in each case.

Stage 4: Chance factors operate for a second time to maintain or change the state of the system, the probabilities and returns being different from those in stage 2.

Stage 5: Once the outcome of stage 4 is known, a final cost is incurred and the process is complete.

What decisions at stage 1 and stage 3 should be made in order to maximise the total expected return? Is this expected return positive, i.e. is the system worth operating?

Solution The probabilities involved in this problem make only a backwards solution possible.

    1   *Stages 4 and 5:* Consider the system as it may be at the end of stage 3 and how stages 4 and 5 could turn out.

If the system is in state *A*, one of two things will happen at random:

either	(i)	it remains in state *A*, with a probability of 0·8 and a return of $+4 - 3 = +1$
or	(ii)	it changes to state *B*, with a probability of 0·2 and a return of $+5 - 2 = +3$.

Thus the expected return during the last two stages of the process will be:

$$(0·8) \times 1 + (0·2) \times 3 = +1·4$$

This would be the total return expected if the system is in state *A* at the end of stage 3. (Expected value was defined in Chapter 2, page 22.)

If the system is in state *B* at the end of stage 3, however,

either	(i)	it remains in state *B*, with a probability of 0·7 and a return of $+6 - 2 = +4$
or	(ii)	it changes to state *A*, with a probability of 0·3 and a return of $+2 - 3 = -1$.

Thus the expected return during the last two stages of the process will be:

$$(0·7) \times 4 - (0·3) \times 1 = +2·5$$

This would be the total return expected if the system is in state *B* at the end of stage 3.

The analysis so far can be represented by the reduced network shown in Fig. 10.4.

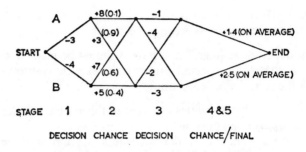

Fig. 10.4 The probabilistic problem, reduced to four stages

2 *Stages 3, 4 and 5:* Now consider the system as it may be at the end of stage 2, either in state A or state B.

If the system is in state A, and if it is decided to maintain it in state A, the return will be $-1 + 1 \cdot 4 = +0 \cdot 4$ on average. If it is decided to change it to state B, then the return will be $-4 + 2 \cdot 5 = -1 \cdot 5$ on average. Therefore it is clearly better to keep it in state A.

If the system is in state B, and if it is decided to maintain it in state B, the return will be $-3 + 2 \cdot 5 = -0 \cdot 5$ on average. If it is decided to change it to state A, then the return will be $-2 + 1 \cdot 4 = -0 \cdot 6$ on average. Therefore it is better to keep it in state B.

The analysis thus far can be represented by a network further reduced, as shown in Fig. 10.5.

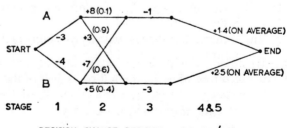

Fig. 10.5 The four-stage problem, further reduced

The best decision to take at stage 3 is not to change the state of the system. This best decision is incorporated in a new network, reduced effectively to three stages, as shown in Fig. 10.6.

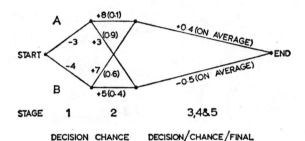

Fig. 10.6 The probabilistic problem, reduced to three stages

3   *Stages 2, 3, 4 and 5:* It is now possible to calculate the expected return from the end of stage 1 to the END, assuming that the optimal decision (not to change state in this case) is made in stage 3.

If the system is in state A, at the end of stage 1, one of two things will happen at random:

either   (i) it remains in state A, with a probability of 0.1 and a return of $+8 + 0.4 = +8.4$

or   (ii) it changes to state B, with a probability of 0.9 and a return of $+3 - 0.5 = +2.5$.

Thus the expected return during the last four stages of the process will be:

$$(0.1) \times 8.4 + (0.9) \times 2.5 = +3.09$$

If the system is in state B at the end of stage 1, however,

either   (i) it remains in state B, with a probability of 0.4 and a return of $+5 - 0.5 = +4.5$

or   (ii) it changes to state A, with a probability of 0.6 and a return of $+7 + 0.4 = +7.4$.

Thus the expected return during the last four stages of the process will be:

$$(0\cdot4) \times 4\cdot5 + (0\cdot6) \times 7\cdot4 = +6\cdot24$$

The network representing this can be reduced to two stages, and is shown in Fig. 10.7.

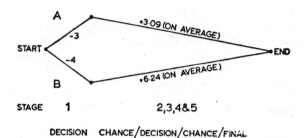

Fig. 10.7　The probabilistic problem, reduced to two stages

4　*All stages:* From Fig. 10.7 it is clear that if state A is selected in stage 1, the total expected return will be $-3 + 3\cdot09 = +0\cdot09$. If state B is selected, however, the total expected return will be $-4 + 6\cdot24 = +2\cdot24$. Therefore, the optimal policy for this system is:

Stage 1 decision: to state B.
Stage 3 decision: do not change state, whether it happens to be A or B at the end of stage 2.

The expected return from this policy will be $+2\cdot24$. Since this expected return is positive, the system is worth operating repeatedly.

Production scheduling and stock control

In introducing some of the ideas of stock control in Chapter 5, we assumed that the demand for a product was constant. The interval between successive production batches was then chosen to make the total cost, of setting up a production run and of stock-holding, as small as possible. When the demand for a product is known exactly but is not the same in each period, the problem of deciding when to produce is more complex. The batches may not be at regular intervals and of the same size in the cheapest schedule. Minimising the sum of production and stock-holding costs, Example 4 illustrates the approach of dynamic programming in deriving the solution to this kind of problem.

EXAMPLE 4

A contract has been signed for the supply of the following number of components at the end of each month:

Month	Month no.	No. of items
April	1	85
May	2	180
June	3	300
July	4	375
August	5	375
September	6	285
		1600 Total

Production during a month is available for supply at the end of the month, or it may be kept in stock for next month or later at a cost of £1 per item per month. The cost of production is £900 per batch and £2 per item.

In what months is a batch to be made, and of what size, if total costs are to be minimised?

Solution Since the production cost per item, £2, is incurred whatever production schedule is adopted, it is a fixed cost of $1600 \times £2 = £3200$ and is irrelevant to the question posed.

If a single batch of 1600 is made in April, the stock levels during the succeeding months are shown below.

May	1515
June	1335
July	1035
August	660
September	285
	4830 Total

Therefore the total stock-holding cost is

$$4830 \times £1 = £4830$$

The cost of the batch is £900, therefore the total cost of this schedule is £5730. At the other extreme, if a batch is made each month and no items are held in stock, the total cost is 6 × £900 = £5400. Some intermediate schedules will have lower total costs than either of these. In order to find which has the lowest, we shall use, as in Example 3, the backwards form of calculation.

6th month: If a batch is made in September, it will cost £900 and there will be no stock left at the end of the month. There will be no stock to carry over from earlier months, since any such items could be made during September at no extra cost and with a saving in stock-holding costs.

Optimal sub-policy (September): make 285, cost £900.

5th month: If a batch is made in August, it will be either

(i) of 375, to be followed by another batch in September, giving a total cost of

$$£900 + £900 = £1800,$$

or

(ii) of 660, with no later batch. This involves a stock-holding cost of £285 and a single batch cost of £900, totalling £1185.

Since (ii) is cheaper than (i),

Optimal sub-policy (August): make 660, none later, cost £1185.

4th month: If a batch is made in July, there are three possibilities:

(i) make 375 now, some more in August
total cost: 900 + 1185 = £2085
(ii) make 750 now, some more in September
total cost: 900 + (1 × 375) + 900 = £2175
(iii) make 1035 now, none later
total cost: 900 + (1 × 375) + (2 × 285) = £1845

Since (iii) is the cheapest, if a batch is made in July it is best not to make any more after that. The second and third elements of the total cost in (iii) represent the stock-holding costs. The second element in (ii) is the stock-holding cost and the third is the optimal sub-policy for September. In (i) the second element is the optimal sub-policy for August. In each case the first element is the cost of the batch in July.

Optimal sub-policy (July): make 1035, none later, cost £1845.

3rd month: If a batch is made in June, there are now four possibilities to be considered, following the same pattern of cost elements as for the 4th month:

 (i) make 300 now, some more in July
      total cost: $900 + 1845 = £2745$
 (ii) make 675 now, some more in August
      total cost: $900 + (1 \times 375) + 1185 = £2460$
(iii) make 1050 now, some more in September
      total cost: $900 + (1 \times 375) + (2 \times 375) + 900 = £2925$
(iv) make 1335 now, none later
      total cost: $900 + (1 \times 375) + (2 \times 275)$
      $$+ (3 \times 385) = £2880$$

Therefore (ii) is the cheapest of these, and:

Optimal sub-policy (June): make 675, more in August, cost £2460

2nd month: If a batch is made in May, the five possibilities are:

 (i) make 180 now, some more in June
      total cost: $900 + 2460 = £3360$
 (ii) make 480 now, some more in July
      total cost: $900 + (1 \times 300) + 1845 = £3045$
(iii) make 855 now, some more in August
      total cost: $900 + (1 \times 300) + (2 \times 375) + 1185 = £3135$
(iv) make 1230 now, some more in September
      total cost: $900 + (1 \times 300) + (2 \times 375)$
      $$+ (3 \times 375) + 900 = £3975$$
 (v) make 1515 now, none later
      total cost: $900 + (1 \times 300) + (2 \times 375)$
      $$+ (3 \times 375) + (4 \times 285) = £4215$$

Therefore (ii) is the cheapest of these, and:

Optimal sub-policy (May): make 480, more in July, cost £3045

1st month: A batch has to be made in April in order to meet at least the demand at the end of the month. There are now six possible decisions about when the next batch should be made.

   (i) make 85 now, some more in May
       total cost: 900 + 3045 = £3945
  (ii) make 265 now, some more in June
       total cost: 900 + (1 × 180) + 2460 = £3540
 (iii) make 565 now, some more in July
       total cost: 900 + (1 × 180) + (2 × 300) + 1845 = £3525
 (iv) make 940 now, some more in August
       total cost: 900 + (1 × 180) + (2 × 300)
                          + (3 × 375) + 1185 = £3990
  (v) make 1315 now, some more in September
       total cost: 900 + (1 × 180) + (2 × 300)
                        + (3 × 375) + (4 × 375) + 900 = £5205
 (vi) make 1600 now, none later
       total cost: 900 + (1 × 180) + (2 × 300)
                      + (3 × 375) + (4 × 375) + (5 × 285) = £5730

Therefore (iii) is the cheapest of these, and:

Optimal policy (April): make 565, more in July, cost £3525

Optimal policy: the optimal schedule is determined by looking at the optimal sub-policies for each month:

If September:	make 285, none later, cost £900
If August:	make 660, none later, cost £1185
If July:	make 1035, none later, cost £1845
If June:	make 675, more in August, cost £2460
If May:	make 480, more in July, cost £3045
If April:	make 565, more in July, cost £3525

Having reached April, during which a batch has to be made, it follows that the best batch size is 565 and the next batch is to be made in July. Now that this is known, the best policy for July is to make 1035 and to have no further batches. Hence the production schedule with the least total cost is:

April:	make 565, for April, May, June
July:	make 1035, for July, August, September

The stock levels in each month are:

April	nil
May	480
June	300
July	nil
August	660
September	285
	1725 Total

Therefore:

Batch cost (×2):	£1800
Stock-holding cost:	£1725
Total cost:	£3525

By the way these calculations have been done, 21 alternatives have been costed. The number of possible alternatives for a six-month schedule is $2^{6-1} = 2^5 = 32$. But if a 12-month schedule had been needed, the dynamic programming method would have involved 66 cases whereas the total possible would have been $2^{12-1} = 2^{11} = 2048$. An example of a 12-month schedule is given in the exercises with a tabulated solution.

Applications of dynamic programming

'An optimal policy has the property that whatever the initial state and initial decision are, the remaining decisions must constitute an optimal policy with regard to the state resulting from the first decision.'

R. E. Bellman

The examples in this chapter have illustrated this principle of optimality. In each case the context has been expressed in terms of routing or scheduling, and the problems have involved discrete variables, e.g. either this route or that route. Applications of dynamic programming with this kind of variable include cargo loading, product standardisation and bidding situations.

Dynamic programming can also be used as a method of approximation when variables are continuous. Applications include water usage, investment analysis and some equipment replacement problems. Intriguing features, both of formulation and computation, arise with such methods, and the bibliography will take the reader further in exploration of them.

Exercises

10.1 (a) Given the network in Fig. 10.2, calculate the backwards solution to the problem of finding the quickest route from *P* to *Z*.

   (b) What are the penalties of taking the wrong route from *P*, given an optimal recovery once the mistake is made?

   (c) What are the optimal sub-routes concerned?

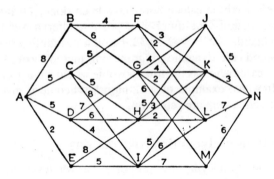

Fig. 10.8 An asymmetric routing problem

10.2 Find the shortest route(s), involving only four arcs, between *A* and *N*, as well as the shortest route(s) from each intermediate city to *N*.

10.3 A manufacturer is committed to supplying the following number of components at the end of each of 12 months:

Month	Month no.	No. of items
October	−5	140
November	−4	170
December	−3	240
January	−2	200
February	−1	150
March	0	100
April	1	85
May	2	180
June	3	300
July	4	375
August	5	375
September	6	285
		2600 Total

The last 6 months' demand is the same as Example 4 in the text; hence the same month numbers have been kept, leading to negative labels from October to February. As before, the cost of a batch is £900 and the stock-holding cost is £1 per item per month.

In what months is a batch to be made, and of what size, if total costs are to be minimised?

Solutions to Exercises

2.1 The simplest reasoning is as follows:
It does not matter what the first card is. What is required is the probability that the second card is

    (*a*) the same colour as the first.
    (*b*) the same suit as the first.

(*a*) The second card could be any of 51 cards,

$$\therefore n = 51$$

25 of these are the same colour as the first,

$$\therefore m = 25$$

Required probability is $\dfrac{m}{n} = \dfrac{25}{51}$

(*b*) Using similar reasoning the required probability is $\dfrac{12}{51}$ or $\dfrac{4}{17}$.

2.2 The possibilities are HTHTH or THTHT.
The probabilities of each of these sequences is $(\frac{1}{2})^5$.
$\therefore$ the required probability is $2 \times (\frac{1}{2})^5$ or $\frac{1}{16}$.

2.3 Think again if you gave the answer as 1. Is it really certain that the ship will be hit? The addition law can only be used when the events are mutually exclusive. Hitting the ship with the first torpedo does not preclude hitting the ship with a later one, and therefore the events are *not* mutually exclusive.
The reasoning should be as follows:
What is the probability that all torpedoes *miss* the ship?
It is the probability that the first misses *and* the second,
third and fourth also miss, i.e. $(\frac{3}{4})^4$ or $\dfrac{81}{256}$

$\therefore$ probability that the ship is hit is $1 - \dfrac{81}{256}$ or $\dfrac{175}{256}$.

2.4 (a) The aircraft crashes if both engines fail.
The probability of this is $(\frac{1}{100})^2$ or 10^{-4}
(b) The aircraft crashes if 3 or 4 engines fail.
This probability is $4(0.01)^3(0.99) + (0.01)^4$ or 3.97×10^{-6}

2.5 Required probability is $20(\frac{1}{2})^3(\frac{1}{2})^3 = \frac{20}{64}$ or $\frac{5}{16}$.

2.6 Mean = 1.5 per day; standard deviation = 1.25. Probabilities given by the Poisson distribution are: $e^{-1.5}$, $1.5e^{-1.5}$, $\dfrac{(1.5)^2}{2} e^{-1.5}$, etc. Multiplying these by 100 we arrive at the following frequencies:

Number requested	Frequency
0	22
1	34
2	25
3	13
4	5
5	1
	100

2.7 A washer is defective if it is less than 2 standard deviations below the mean or greater than 1.2 standard deviations above the mean.
Probability of a value greater than 2 standard deviations from the mean is $1 - 0.977$ (from Table 2.6) = 0.023. Probability of a value greater than 1.2 standard deviations from the mean is $1 - 0.885 = 0.115$. Probability of being outside the tolerance is $0.023 + 0.115 = 0.138$. Therefore the percentage of defective washers produced is 13.8.

3.1 (i) If the cost per bulb of group replacement increases to £1, then clearly individual replacement will be cheaper than any group replacement policy. The cost of the policies examined will be:

	Group	+	Individual		Total cost, £		Cost per week
(a)	100	+	0	=	100	or	£100
(b)	100	+	30	=	130		£65
(c)	100	+	109	=	209		£69$\frac{2}{3}$
(d)			59	=	59		£59

The cost of these policies with group replacement at £0·50 per bulb were:

(a) £50 per week   (b) £40 per week
(c) £53 per week   (d) £59 per week

It follows, therefore, with the cost per bulb of group replacement in the range £0·50 to £1·00, policy (b) is always better than policy (a) and policy (c). Hence it is necessary to consider only when policy (b) becomes more expensive than policy (d).

(ii) If the cost per bulb of group replacement rises from £0·50 to £0·88, the cost of policy (b) becomes:

$$\frac{88 + 30}{2} = £59 \text{ per week}$$

Therefore, if the cost per bulb of group replacement rises above £0·88, then individual replacement will be cheaper than group replacement policy (b), and hence also cheaper than policies (a) and (c).

3.2 (i) *£0·59 per bulb*, group replacement:

	Group	+	Individual		Total cost, £		Cost per week
(a)	59	+	0	=	59	or	£59
(b)	59	+	30	=	89		£44·5
(c)	59	+	109	=	168		£56
(d)			59	=	59		£59

(ii) *£0·68 per bulb*, group replacement:

	Group	+	Individual		Total cost, £		Cost per week
(a)	68	+	0	=	68	or	£68
(b)	68	+	30	=	98		£49
(c)	68	+	109	=	177		£59
(d)			59	=	59		£59

3.3

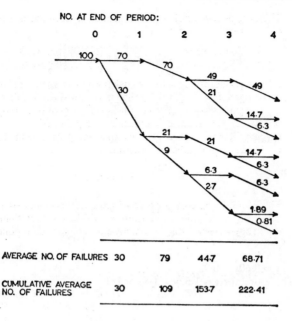

NO. AT END OF PERIOD:

Extended failure tree (Example 1)

3.4

Year no.	No. of original staff employed at end of year	Survival probability	Resignation probability
0	1000	1·00	
1	940	0·94	0·06
2	820	0·82	0·12
3	580	0·58	0·24
4	400	0·40	0·18
5	280	0·28	0·12
6	190	0·19	0·09
7	130	0·13	0·06
8	70	0·07	0·06
9	30	0·03	0·04
10	0	0·00	0·03
		Total	1·00

The resignation probabilities are the differences between successive survival probabilities.

4.1

x	y	x^2	xy
1·9	2·2	3·61	4·18
2·5	2·3	6·25	5·75
0·8	1·3	0·64	1·04
1·9	1·8	3·61	3·42
1·2	2·0	1·44	2·40
2·7	2·7	7·29	7·29
1·4	1·6	1·96	2·24

Totals 12·4   13·9   24·80   26·32

$$n = 7$$

$$m = \frac{7 \times 26 \cdot 32 - 12 \cdot 4 \times 13 \cdot 9}{7 \times 24 \cdot 80 - 12 \cdot 4 \times 12 \cdot 4} = \frac{11 \cdot 88}{19 \cdot 84} = 0 \cdot 60$$

$$c = \frac{13 \cdot 9 - 0 \cdot 6 \times 12 \cdot 4}{7} = \frac{6 \cdot 46}{7} = 0 \cdot 92$$

$$\therefore y = 0 \cdot 60x + 0 \cdot 92$$

Therefore, for $x = 1 \cdot 6$, $y = 1 \cdot 88$ or $1 \cdot 9$

4.2 *Error*   *Probability*

x	p	px	px^2
−1	0·6	−0·6	0·6
0	0·1	0	0
+1	0·1	+0·1	0·1
+2	0·1	+0·2	0·4
+3	0·1	+0·3	0·9
		$\Sigma px = 0$	$\Sigma px^2 = 2 \cdot 0$

Mean = $\Sigma px = 0$

Standard deviation = $\sqrt{\Sigma px^2} = \sqrt{2 \cdot 0} = 1 \cdot 4$

4.3

$$\frac{29 + 24 + 29 + 34 + 29}{5} = 29$$

$$\frac{24 + 29 + 34 + 29 + 24}{5} = 28$$

$$\frac{29 + 34 + 29 + 24 + 29}{5} = 29$$

$$\frac{34 + 29 + 24 + 29 + 34}{5} = 30$$

$$\frac{29 + 24 + 29 + 34 + 29}{5} = 29 \text{ again, and so on.}$$

Also

$$\frac{29 + 24 + 29 + 34 + 29 + 24}{6} = 28\tfrac{1}{6}$$

$$\frac{24 + 29 + 34 + 29 + 24 + 29}{6} = 28\tfrac{1}{6}$$

$$\frac{29 + 34 + 29 + 24 + 29 + 34}{6} = 29\tfrac{5}{6}$$

$$\frac{34 + 29 + 24 + 29 + 34 + 29}{6} = 29\tfrac{5}{6}$$

$$\frac{29 + 24 + 29 + 34 + 29 + 24}{6} = 28\tfrac{1}{6} \text{ again, and so on.}$$

4.4 Coefficients are:

$$\alpha$$
$$\alpha(1 - \alpha)$$
$$\alpha(1 - \alpha)^2 \text{ etc.}$$

Now, $\dfrac{1}{1 - x} = 1 + x + x^2 + x^3 + \dots$

shown by long division of $(1 - x)$ into 1.

Therefore the sum of the coefficients:

$$\alpha + \alpha(1 - \alpha) + \alpha(1 - \alpha)^2 + \dots$$
$$= \alpha(1 + (1 - \alpha)) + (1 - \alpha)^2 + \dots$$

$$= \alpha \left(\frac{1}{1 - (1 - \alpha)} \right) = \alpha \left(\frac{1}{\alpha} \right) = 1$$

Hence F_0 is a properly constructed weighted average.

4.5

Observation	Forecast	Error	$\frac{1}{5}$ Error	New forecast
30	30	0	0	30
35	30	+5	+1	31
30	31	−1	−0·2	30·8
30	30·8	−0·8	−0·16	30·64
30	30·64	−0·64	−0·13	30·51
30	30·51	−0·51	−0·10	30·41
30	30·41	−0·41	−0·08	30·33
30	30·33	−0·33	−0·06	30·27
30	30·27	−0·27	−0·05	30·22
.	30·22			
.				
.				

4.6

Observation	Forecast	Error	$\frac{1}{5}$ Error	New forecast
30	30	0	0	30
30	30	0	0	30
30	30	0	0	30
35	30	+5	+1	31
35	31	+4	+0·8	31·8
35	31·8	+3·2	+0·64	32·44
35	32·44	+2·56	+0·51	32·95
35	32·95	+2·05	+0·41	33·36
35	33·36	+1·64	+0·33	33·69
.	33·69			
.				
.				

5.1

d = 13 500 per year
r = 135 000 per year
p = £15
i = 0·2
c = £10 000

$$Q = \sqrt{\dfrac{2 \times 13\,500 \times 10\,000}{0\cdot2 \times 15 \left(1 - \dfrac{13\,500}{135\,000}\right)}} = 10\,000.$$

Set-up cost per unit = £ $\dfrac{10\,000}{10\,000}$ = £1

Stock-holding cost per unit

$$= £ \left[\frac{0 \cdot 2 \times 15 \times 5000 \left(1 - \frac{13\,500}{135\,000} \right)}{13\,500} \right]$$

$$= £1$$

Total costs per piece = (fixed cost + set-up cost + stock-holding cost) per piece = £17

5.2 When the economic batch quantity is produced the stock-holding cost per piece equals the set-up cost per piece = x, say.

The total variable cost = $2x$.

When the batch size is doubled, the stock-holding cost per piece is doubled, whilst the set-up cost per piece is halved.

The new total variable cost is, therefore, $2x + \dfrac{x}{2} = \dfrac{5x}{2}$,

i.e. an increase of 25%.

As the variable cost makes up 20% of total costs, the increase in total cost is 5%. Similar reasoning shows that the effect of halving the batch size is identical to the effect of doubling it.

5.3 The following is a Poisson distribution with a mean of 2:

Demand	Probability
0	0·14
1	0·27
2	0·27
3	0·18
4	0·09
5	0·04
6	0·01
	1·00

Let x be the number of pieces of equipment the contractor has on long-term hire. The optimum value of x is the lowest which satisfies the following inequality:

Probability that the demand exceeds $x \leqslant \dfrac{h}{h+s}$.

h is the cost of holding an item which is not required, i.e. £10; s is the cost of not holding an item which is required. This is the difference between the costs of having and operating equipment on long- and short-term hire, i.e. £50 − £30 = £20

$$\frac{h}{h + s} = \frac{1}{3}$$

Probability that the demand exceeds 2 pieces of equipment is 0·18 + 0·09 + 0·04 + 0·01 = 0·32. This is the lowest value of x for which the probability of needing more than $x \leqslant \frac{1}{3}$. Therefore two pieces of equipment should be obtained on long-term hire.

This problem may be solved by enumeration as follows:

The table below gives the daily cost (£) for all possible combinations of the number of pieces of equipment,

(*a*) held on long-term hire; and
(*b*) required.

Number held on long-term hire

		0	1	2	3	4	5	6
	0	0	10	20	30	40	50	60
	1	50	30	40	50	60	70	80
	2	100	80	60	70	80	90	100
Number required	3	150	130	110	90	100	110	120
	4	200	180	160	140	120	130	140
	5	250	230	210	190	170	150	160
	6	300	280	260	240	220	200	180

Because we know the probability distribution of demand, we may calculate the expected cost attached to holding any number of pieces of equipment on long-term hire. The expected cost attached to holding none on long-term hire is given below:

Demand	Cost	Probability of this demand	
	x	p	px
0	0	0·14	0
1	50	0·27	13·5
2	100	0·27	27·0
3	150	0·18	27·0
4	200	0·09	18·0
5	250	0·04	10·0
6	300	0·01	3·0

Expected cost = $\Sigma px =$ 98·5

A similar calculation can be performed for all possible holdings on long-term hire. These expected costs are given below:

Number held on long-term hire	Expected daily cost (£)
0	98·5
1	82·7
2	75·0
3	75·4
4	81·2
5	89·7
6	99·4

The lowest daily cost corresponds to holding 2 items on long-term hire.

5.4 Demand $\qquad\qquad d = 30$ tons/year
Ordering cost $\qquad c = £100$
Stock-holding cost $\qquad i = 0·2$ p.a.
Price $\qquad\qquad\quad p = £300$

Economic batch quantity = $\sqrt{\dfrac{2cd}{ip}} = 10$ tons

Ordering is carried out 3 times a year on average.

To run out of stock once in 5 years implies a probability per occasion of $\frac{1}{15}$ or 0·067.

To achieve this probability of stock-out the company should cater for the expected usage plus 1·5 standard deviations of the forecast error. The re-order level should be 2·75 + 0·75 or 3·5 tons.

6.1 (a) Traffic intensity less than 1, or
         mean rate of arrival < mean rate of service.
   (b) The average length of the queue increases indefinitely.

6.2

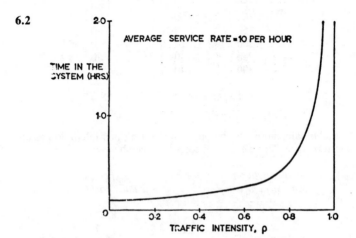

How the average time a customer is in the system depends on traffic intensity

6.3 (i) For a single channel, with $\lambda = 22$ and $\mu = 23$ per hour; the traffic intensity = 22/23, and average time in the system

$$= \left(\frac{1}{1 - \dfrac{22}{23}}\right) \frac{1}{23}$$

$$= \left(\frac{23}{23 - 22}\right) \frac{1}{23}$$

$$= 1 \text{ hour}$$

   (ii) For two channels, with $\lambda = 22$ and $\mu = 12$ per hour at each channel, the traffic intensity = 22/24, and average time in the system

$$= \frac{(2\varrho)^2}{2(1 - \varrho)^2 \, 2\mu} \; \frac{2(1 - \varrho)}{(2\varrho)^2 + 2(1 - \varrho)\{1 + 2\varrho\}} \; + \frac{1}{\mu}$$

$$= \frac{\varrho^2}{(1 - \varrho)\mu(2\varrho^2 + 1 + \varrho - 2\varrho^2)} + \frac{1}{\mu}$$

$$= \frac{\varrho^2}{\mu(1 - \varrho)(1 + \varrho)} + \frac{1}{\mu}$$

$$= \frac{(22/24)^2}{12\left(1 - \dfrac{22}{24}\right)\left(1 + \dfrac{22}{24}\right)} + \frac{1}{12}$$

$$= \frac{22^2}{12(24 - 22)(24 + 22)} + \frac{1}{12}$$

$$= \frac{22 \times 22}{12 \times 2 \times 46} + \frac{1}{12}$$

$$= \frac{484 + 92}{12 \times 2 \times 46} = \frac{12}{23} \text{ hours}$$

$$= 0\cdot52 \text{ hours}$$

Thus, these two channels in parallel ($\mu = 12$) give a better service than a single channel ($\mu = 23$). If the performance of the single channel could be improved to serve 23·92 or more per hour, then its service would become better than the two channels in parallel ($\mu = 12$).

7.1 Let x_1 be the number of dolls of type A produced per day and x_2 ,, ,, ,, ,, ,, ,, ,, B ,, ,, ,,
The linear programming formulation is as follows:

Maximise:	$3x_1 + 5x_2$
subject to	$x_1 \geq 0$
	$x_2 \geq 0$
and	$x_1 + 2x_2 \leq 2000$ (time constraint)
	$x_1 + x_2 \leq 1500$ (plastic ,,)
	$x_2 \leq 600$ (dress ,,)
Solution:	$x_1 = 1000; \quad x_2 = 500$
	Profit = £5500

7.2   Let x_1 be the number of metres of tweed A produced
and x_2 ,, ,, ,, ,, ,, ,, ,, B ,,
The linear programming formulation is:

Maximise: $2x_1 + 4x_2$
subject to $x_1 \geq 0$
                                        $x_2 \geq 0$

and

$$160x_1 + 200x_2 \leq 1\,600\,000 \quad \text{(grey wool constraint)}$$
$$50x_1 + 20x_2 \leq 400\,000 \quad \text{(red \quad ,, \qquad ,, \quad)}$$
$$40x_1 + 80x_2 \leq 600\,000 \quad \text{(green ,, \qquad ,, \quad)}$$
$$x_1 + x_2 \leq 9000 \quad \text{(machine constraint)}$$
$$x_1 \geq 3000 \quad \text{(sales constraint)}$$

Solution:
(a) $x_1 = 3000$; $x_2 = 5600$
    Profit = £28 400
(b) Either
    $x_1 = 1667$; $x_2 = 6667$
    or
    $x_1 = 0$; $x_2 = 7500$
    or, in fact, $x_1 = 1667\lambda$; $x_2 = 6667\lambda + 7500(1 - \lambda)$
    (where λ may take any value between 0 and 1).

New profit = £30 000, i.e. an increase of £1600.

NB. The reason for the multiplicity of solutions to (b) is that the objective function is parallel to one of the edges of the feasible region.

7.3   Let x_1 be the no. of kgs of food   I used in the diet
x_2 ,, ,, ,, ,, ,, ,, ,,   II ,, ,, ,, ,,
x_3 ,, ,, ,, ,, ,, ,, ,,   III ,, ,, ,, ,,
x_4 ,, ,, ,, ,, ,, ,, ,,   IV ,, ,, ,, ,,

The linear programming formulation is as follows:

Minimise: $40x_1 + 20x_2 + 50x_3 + 60x_4$
subject to $x_1 \geq 0$
                                        $x_2 \geq 0$
                                        $x_3 \geq 0$
                                        $x_4 \geq 0$

and $600x_1 + 50x_2 + 500x_3 + 800x_4 \geq 3000$
              $2x_1 + 8x_2 + 10x_3 + 3x_4 \geq 80$

7.4

	Route *aA*	1 bus
	bA	1 bus
	bB	5 buses
	bC	2 buses
	cC	7 buses

Total distance travelled: 112 kilometres.

7.5 From the network the rail distance (kilometres) between collieries and coke ovens can be shown to be as follows:

	a	*b*	*c*	*d*
A	10	13	14	20
B	7	8	29	23
C	28	27	16	14

Solution:

	Route *aA*	1000	tons/month
	aB	2000	,,
	bB	2000	,,
	cA	1000	,,
	cC	3000	,,
	dC	3000	,,

Total cost per month: £7200

7.6 Optimal assignment is:

$$A - X, B - W, C - V, D - Y \text{ and } E - Z$$

Total number of man-hours is 45.

7.7 Let x_{AV} be 1 (if job A is performed by subordinate V) or 0 (if job A is not performed by subordinate V) and similarly for $x_{AW}, x_{AX}, \ldots, x_{EZ}$.

Minimise:

$$
\begin{aligned}
&3x_{AV} + 5x_{AW} + 10x_{AX} + 15x_{AY} + 8x_{AZ} \\
&+4x_{BV} + 7x_{BW} + 15x_{BX} + 18x_{BY} + 8x_{BZ} \\
&+8x_{CV} + 12x_{CW} + 20x_{CX} + 20x_{CY} + 12x_{CZ} \\
&+5x_{DV} + 5x_{DW} + 8x_{DX} + 10x_{DY} + 6x_{DZ} \\
&+10x_{EV} + 10x_{EW} + 15x_{EX} + 25x_{EY} + 10x_{EZ}
\end{aligned}
$$

subject to:
$$x_{AV} + x_{AW} + x_{AX} + x_{AY} + x_{AZ} = 1$$
$$x_{BV} + x_{BW} + x_{BX} + x_{BY} + x_{BZ} = 1$$
$$x_{CV} + x_{CW} + x_{CX} + x_{CY} + x_{CZ} = 1$$
$$x_{DV} + x_{DW} + x_{DX} + x_{DY} + x_{DZ} = 1$$
$$x_{EV} + x_{EW} + x_{EX} + x_{EY} + x_{EZ} = 1$$

$$x_{AV} + x_{BV} + x_{CV} + x_{DV} + x_{EV} = 1$$
$$x_{AW} + x_{BW} + x_{CW} + x_{DW} + x_{EW} = 1$$
$$x_{AX} + x_{BX} + x_{CX} + x_{DX} + x_{EX} = 1$$
$$x_{AY} + x_{BY} + x_{CY} + x_{DY} + x_{EY} = 1$$
$$x_{AZ} + x_{BZ} + x_{CZ} + x_{DZ} + x_{EZ} = 1$$

The linear programming formulation of Example 2:
Let

x_{aA} be the amount sent from warehouse a to customer A
x_{aB} ,, ,, ,, ,, ,, ,, a ,, ,, B
etc.

Minimise
$$8x_{aA} + 9x_{bA} + 6x_{cA} + 3x_{dA} + 6x_{aB} + 11x_{bB} + 5x_{cB} + 10x_{dB}$$
$$+ 3x_{aC} + 8x_{bC} + 7x_{cC} + 9x_{dC}$$
$$\dots \text{(objective function)} \tag{9}$$

subject to
$$\left. \begin{array}{l} x_{aA} \geq 0 \\ x_{bA} \geq 0 \\ \cdot \\ \cdot \\ \cdot \\ x_{dC} \geq 0 \end{array} \right\} \tag{10}$$

and
$$\left. \begin{array}{l} x_{aA} + x_{aB} + x_{aC} = 15 \\ x_{bA} + x_{bB} + x_{bC} = 16 \\ x_{cA} + x_{cB} + x_{cC} = 11 \\ x_{dA} + x_{dB} + x_{dC} = 13 \\ x_{aA} + x_{bA} + x_{cA} + x_{dA} = 17 \\ x_{aB} + x_{bB} + x_{cB} + x_{dB} = 20 \\ x_{aC} + x_{bC} + x_{cC} + x_{dC} = 18 \end{array} \right\} \tag{11}$$

NB. As the number of units available equals the number required, the equations (11) replace the more general inequalities.

8.1   The game has a saddle point. A plays I throughout, B plays I throughout, $v = 1$.

8.2   The game has a saddle point. A plays III throughout, B plays II throughout, $v = 2$.

8.3 After elimination of recessive courses of action the pay-off matrix is reduced to:

$$\begin{array}{cc} & \textit{Player B} \\ & \begin{array}{cc} \text{I} & \text{II} \end{array} \\ \textit{Player A} \begin{array}{c} \text{II} \\ \text{III} \end{array} & \begin{bmatrix} 2 & -1 \\ -1 & 0 \end{bmatrix} \end{array}$$

A plays $(0, \frac{1}{4}, \frac{3}{4}, 0)$, B plays $(\frac{1}{4}, \frac{3}{4}, 0)$, $v = -\frac{1}{4}$.

8.4 After elimination of recessive course of action the pay-off matrix becomes:

$$\begin{array}{cc} & \textit{Player B} \\ & \begin{array}{ccc} \text{I} & \text{II} & \text{III} \end{array} \\ \textit{Player A} \begin{array}{c} \text{II} \\ \text{III} \end{array} & \begin{bmatrix} 4 & 0 & 2 \\ -5 & 2 & 0 \end{bmatrix} \end{array}$$

A plays $(0, \frac{7}{11}, \frac{4}{11})$, B plays $(\frac{2}{11}, \frac{9}{11}, 0)$, $v = \frac{8}{11}$.

8.5 The pay-off matrix is:

		Non-matching player	
		I (Heads)	II (Tails)
Matching player	I (Heads)	£8	−£3
	II (Tails)	−£3	£1

The value of the game is $-\frac{1}{15}$ to the matching player. The non-matching player thus guarantees an average gain of £$\frac{1}{15}$, i.e. just under 7p per play, if he plays $(\frac{4}{15}, \frac{11}{15})$.

8.6 If the problem is solved graphically all the lines intersect at the point $y = \frac{2}{3}$, $g = \frac{1}{3}$.

Player A has six equally good strategies:

$(\frac{1}{3}, 0, 0, \frac{2}{3}, 0)$, $(\frac{1}{9}, 0, 0, 0, \frac{8}{9})$, $(0, \frac{2}{3}, 0, \frac{1}{3}, 0)$, $(0, \frac{1}{3}, 0, 0, \frac{2}{3})$, $(0, 0, \frac{4}{9}, \frac{5}{9}, 0)$, $(0, 0, \frac{1}{6}, 0, \frac{5}{6})$

The value of the game is $\frac{1}{3}$.

8.7 The pay-off matrix is:

$$\begin{array}{cc} & \textit{Player B} \\ & \begin{array}{cc} \text{I} & \text{II} \\ \text{`A'} & \text{`I'} \end{array} \\ \textit{Player A} \begin{array}{ccc} \text{I} & \text{`KN'} \\ \text{II} & \text{`KR'} \\ \text{III} & \text{`NR'} \end{array} & \begin{bmatrix} -3 & 3 \\ 1 & 1 \\ 2 & -3 \end{bmatrix} \end{array}$$

The game is best solved graphically, yielding the pure strategy II throughout as the best strategy for player *A*. The value of the game is 1. The optimum strategy for player *B* is to choose 'A' with a probability of not less than $\frac{1}{3}$ and not greater than $\frac{4}{5}$. If this probability is less than $\frac{1}{3}$, player *A* could increase his gain by choosing 'KN'; if it is greater than $\frac{4}{5}$ he could increase his gain by choosing 'NR'.

9.1

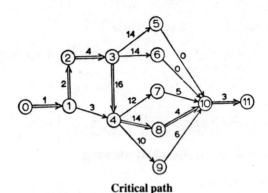

Critical path

Critical activities: double lines
Project duration: 44 days

9.2   Eight.

9.3

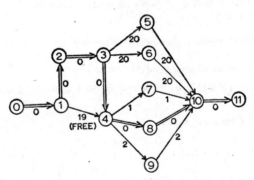

Activity floats

All floats interfering except 1–4, marked 'free'
Sub-critical activities: 4–7, 7–10 float 1
                        4–9, 9–10 float 2

9.4 One of several minor variants of the manpower schedule is:

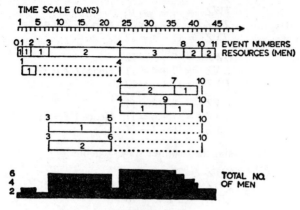

Manpower schedule

9.5 Yes.

When there are only five men available, and with two men on 4–7 and three men on 4–8 from day 24, it is impossible to start 4–9 at the same time. This activity cannot start until 4–7 is completed, releasing the two men on day 36. Thus this activity becomes 7–9, and 4–7 is deleted. The network that results has the following events on the new critical path:

$$0, 1, 2, 3, 4, 7, 9, 10, 11$$

The project duration is 54 days.
The new floats are:

1–4 : 19	free	
3–5 : 30	⎫	
5–10: 30		
3–6 : 30		
6–10: 30	⎬ interfering	
4–8 : 10		
8–10: 10	⎭	
7–10: 11	free	

10.1 (*a*) Let the *quickest* route between any two cities be referred only by the initial and terminal cities concerned.

(4) Starting with the last stage:

$$WZ = 3$$
$$XZ = 1$$
$$YZ = 1$$

(3) Incorporating the penultimate stage:

$$
\begin{aligned}
TWZ &= 7 + 3 = 10 \\
TXZ &= 5 + 4 = 9 \quad \text{Hence } TZ = 9 \\
TYZ &= 11 + 1 = 12
\end{aligned}
$$

$$
\begin{aligned}
UWZ &= 9 + 3 = 12 \\
UXZ &= 7 + 4 = 11 \quad \text{Hence } UZ = 11 \\
UYZ &= 11 + 1 = 12
\end{aligned}
$$

$$
\begin{aligned}
VWZ &= 8 + 3 = 11 \\
VXZ &= 7 + 4 = 11 \quad \text{Hence } VZ = 11 \\
VYZ &= 10 + 1 = 11
\end{aligned}
$$

(2) Taking the last three stages together:

$$
\begin{aligned}
QTZ &= 7 + 9 = 16 \\
QUZ &= 6 + 11 = 17 \quad \text{Hence } QZ = 16 \\
QVZ &= 5 + 11 = 16
\end{aligned}
$$

$$
\begin{aligned}
RTZ &= 8 + 9 = 17 \\
RUZ &= 5 + 11 = 16 \quad \text{Hence } RZ = 16 \\
RVZ &= 7 + 11 = 18
\end{aligned}
$$

$$
\begin{aligned}
STZ &= 4 + 9 = 13 \\
SUZ &= 4 + 11 = 15 \quad \text{Hence } SZ = 13 \\
SVZ &= 6 + 11 = 17
\end{aligned}
$$

(1) Finally the quickest overall route is given by:

$$
\begin{aligned}
PQZ &= 3 + 16 = 19 \\
PRZ &= 1 + 16 = 17 \quad \text{Hence } PZ = 16 \\
PSZ &= 3 + 13 = 16
\end{aligned}
$$

The quickest route PZ was PSZ, see (1).
The quickest route SZ was STZ, see (2).
The quickest route TZ was TXZ, see (3).
The quickest route XZ was XZ, see (4).
Hence the quickest route is $PSTXZ$, with a total time of 16.

(b) If, instead of going from P to S etc. we go to Q, the quickest sub-route $QZ = 16$. Thus the total time is $PQ + QZ = 3 + 16 = 19$, which is 3 more than PZ. If we go to R, the quickest sub-route $RZ = 16$. Thus the total time is $PR + RZ = 1 + 16 = 17$, which is 1 more than PZ.

(c) QZ was either via T or via V.

$$
\begin{aligned}
\text{If } T,\ TZ \text{ was via } X, \text{ and } QZ &= QTXZ \\
\text{If } V,\ TZ \text{ was via } W, \text{ and } QZ &= QVWZ \\
\text{or via } X, \text{ and } QZ &= QVXZ \\
\text{or via } Y, \text{ and } QZ &= QVYZ
\end{aligned}
$$

Thus there happen to be four equally optimal recoveries from Q, only one of which is returning to the originally optimal route via TXZ.

RZ was via U, UZ was via X, and so $RZ = RUXZ$

Thus there is only one optimal recovery from R, which does not join the originally optimal route until X.

With the other numbers on each route, it might be that an optimal recovery from a mistake does not include any of the originally optimal route. Reverting to what remains of the original route may even be the worst response.

10.2 (4)
$$JN = 5 \quad LN = 7$$
$$KN = 3 \quad MN = 6$$

(3) Incorporating the penultimate stage:

$$FKN = 3 + 3 = 6 \quad \text{Hence } FN = 6$$
$$FLN = 2 + 7 = 9$$

$$GJN = 4 + 5 = 9$$
$$GKN = 4 + 3 = 7 \quad \text{Hence } GN = 7$$
$$GLN = 2 + 7 = 9$$
$$GMN = 6 + 6 = 12$$

$$HJN = 5 + 5 = 10$$
$$HKN = 3 + 3 = 6 \quad \text{Hence } HN = 6$$
$$HLN = 2 + 7 = 9$$

$$IKN = 5 + 3 = 8 \quad \text{Hence } IN = 8$$
$$ILN = 6 + 7 = 13$$
$$IMN = 7 + 6 = 13$$

(2) Taking the last three stages together:

$$BFN = 4 + 6 = 10 \quad \text{Hence } BN = 10$$
$$BGN = 6 + 7 = 13$$

$$\left.\begin{array}{l} CFN = 5 + 6 = 11 \\ CHN = 5 + 6 = 11 \end{array}\right\} \quad \text{Hence } CN = 11$$
$$CIN = 8 + 8 = 16$$

$$\left.\begin{array}{l} DGN = 7 + 7 = 14 \\ DHN = 6 + 6 = 12 \\ DIN = 4 + 8 = 12 \end{array}\right\} \quad \text{Hence } DN = 12$$

$$EHN = 8 + 6 = 14$$
$$EIN = 5 + 8 = 13 \quad \text{Hence } EN = 13$$

(1) Finally the best route is given by:

$$ABN = 8 + 10 = 18$$
$$ACN = 5 + 11 = 16$$
$$ADN = 5 + 12 = 17$$
$$AEN = 2 + 13 = 15 \quad \text{Hence } AN = 15$$

The shortest routes from all cities to N, together with the relevant total distance in brackets, are given in the network below.

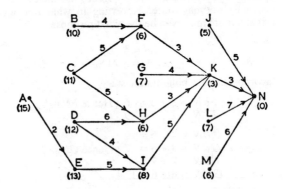

Solution to the asymmetric routing problem

10.3 In the table overleaf the following symbols are used:

CC = cumulative costs of making a batch now and of holding stock until the next batch is made.

OSP = cost of optimal sub-policy, when the next batch is made and thereafter.

SP = cost of sub-policy, the sum of CC + OSP.

In each row of SP, the smallest entry is the new OSP, shown in bold type. In the SP row for the initial month (-5), the smallest entry is the overall minimum total cost.

The optimal policy and sub-policies, the batch sizes and the total costs are shown in the diagram opposite.

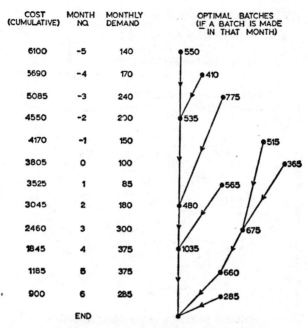

COST (CUMULATIVE)	MONTH NO.	MONTHLY DEMAND	OPTIMAL BATCHES (IF A BATCH IS MADE IN THAT MONTH)
6100	-5	140	550
5690	-4	170	410
5085	-3	240	775
4550	-2	200	535
4170	-1	150	515
3805	0	100	365
3525	1	85	565
3045	2	180	480
2460	3	300	675
1845	4	375	1035
1185	5	375	660
900	6	285	285
	END		

Solution to the production scheduling problem

The diagram shows that the optimal policy is:

Make 550: October (-5)
535: January (-2)
480: May (2)
1035: July (4)

If a batch cannot be produced in one of these months, that month's demand must be met by buying from an outside supplier. The best reaction to such a situation is also shown in the diagram by the optimal sub-policies. Thus if production is delayed from October until December, it is better to make a large batch (775) then and no more until May, rather than make 240 in December and the January batch of 535 as originally planned.

Complete tabulation of the solution to Exercise 10.3

Now (month no.)		No. of months in stock between now and the next batch												Now (month no.)
		0	1	2	3	4	5	6	7	8	9	10	11	
6	CC	900												6
	OSP	–												
	SP	**900**												
5	CC	900	1185											5
	OSP	900	–											
	SP	1800	**1185**											
4	CC	900	1275	1845										4
	OSP	1185	900	–										
	SP	2085	2175	**1845**										
3	CC	900	1275	2025	2880									3
	OSP	1845	1185	900	–									
	SP	2745	**2460**	2925	2880									
2	CC	900	1200	1950	3075	4215								2
	OSP	2460	1845	1185	900	–								
	SP	3360	**3045**	3135	3975	4215								
1	CC	900	1080	1680	2805	4305	5730							1
	OSP	3045	2460	1845	1185	900	–							
	SP	3945	3540	**3525**	3990	5205	5730							

								0	−1	−2	−3	−4	−5
0	CC	900	985	1345	2245	3745	5620	7330					
	OSP	3525	3045	2460	1845	1185	900	–					
	SP	4425	4030	**3805**	4090	4930	6520	7330					
−1	CC	900	1000	1170	1710	2910	4785	7035	9030				
	OSP	3805	3525	3045	2460	1845	1185	900	–				
	SP	4705	4525	4215	**4170**	4755	5970	7935	9030				
−2	CC	900	1050	1250	1505	2225	3725	5975	8600	10880			
	OSP	4170	3805	3525	3045	2460	1845	1185	900	–			
	SP	5070	4855	4775	**4550**	4685	5570	7160	9500	10880			
−3	CC	900	1100	1400	1700	2040	2940	4740	7365	10365	12930		
	OSP	4550	4170	3805	3525	3045	2460	1845	1185	900	–		
	SP	5450	5270	5205	5225	**5085**	5400	6585	8550	11265	12930		
−4	CC	900	1140	1540	1990	2390	2815	3895	5995	8995	12370	15220	
	OSP	5085	4550	4170	3805	3525	3045	2460	1845	1185	900	–	
	SP	5985	**5690**	5710	5795	5915	5860	6355	7840	10180	13270	15220	
−5	CC	900	1070	1550	2150	2750	3250	3760	5020	7420	10795	14545	17680
	OSP	5690	5085	4550	4170	3805	3525	3045	2460	1845	1185	900	–
	SP	6590	6155	**6100**	6320	6555	6775	6805	7480	9265	11980	15445	17680

Bibliography

Chapter 1 Operational Research

Dyer, J. S. and Shapiro, R. D., *Management Science and Operations Research: Cases and Readings* (1982), John Wiley and Sons.

Eden, C., Jones, S. and Sims, D., *Messing About in Problems* (1983), Pergamon Press.

Fabrycky, W. J., Ghare, P. M. and Torgersen, P. E., *Applied Operations Research and Management Science* (1984), Prentice-Hall International.

Gregory, G., *Mathematical Methods in Management* (1984), John Wiley and Sons.

Jeffers, J. N. R., *An Introduction to Systems Analysis: with Ecological Applications* (1978), Edward Arnold.

Markland, R. E., *Topics in Management Science* (2nd ed. 1983), John Wiley and Sons.

Saaty, T. L. and Alexander, J. M., *Thinking with Models* (1981), Pergamon Press.

Wilkes, F. M., *Elements of Operational Research* (1980), McGraw-Hill.

Chapter 2 Probability

Hertz, D. B. and Thomas, H., *Risk Analysis and Its Applications* (1983), John Wiley and Sons.

Targett, D., *Coping with Numbers* (1984), Martin Robertson and Co.

Chapter 3 Replacement

Eglese, R. W. and Rand, G. K. (eds.), *Developments in Operational Research* (1984), Pergamon Press.

Gheorghe, A., *Applied Systems Engineering* (1982), John Wiley and Sons.

Kaufmann, A., *Methods and Models of Operations Research* (1963), Prentice-Hall International.

Sussams, J. E., *Vehicle Replacement* (1983), Gower Press.

Chapter 4 Forecasting

Makridakis, S., Wheelwright, S. C. and McGee, V. E., *Forecasting: Methods and Applications* (2nd ed. 1983), John Wiley and Sons.

O'Donovan, T. M., *Short-Term Forecasting: An Introduction to the Box-Jenkins Approach* (1983), John Wiley and Sons.

Chapter 5 Stock Control

Bensoussan, A., Crouhy, M. and Proth, J.-M., *Mathematical Theory of Production Planning* (1984), North-Holland.

Hill, T., *Production Operations Management* (1983), Prentice-Hall International.

Chapter 6 Queues

Chaudhry, M. L. and Templeton, J. C. C., *A First Course in Bulk Queues* (1983), Wiley Interscience.

Pritsker, A. A. B. and Sigal, C. E., *Management Decision Models: A Network Simulation Approach* (1983), Prentice-Hall International.

Stoyan, D., *Comparison Methods for Queues and Other Stochastic Models* (1984), John Wiley and Sons.

Chapter 7 Linear Programming

Kaplan, E. L., *Review of Mathematical Programming and Games* (1982), John Wiley and Sons.

White, D. J., Donaldson, W. A. and Lawrie, N. L., *Operational Research Techniques: Volume 1* (1969), Business Books.

Chapter 8 Theory of Games

Bunn, D. W., *Applied Decision Analysis* (1984), McGraw-Hill.

Colman, A. M., *Game Theory and Experimental Games: The Study of Strategic Interaction* (1982), Pergamon Press.

Kacprzyk, J., *Multistage Decision-Making under Fuzziness* (1983), Verlag T.U.V. Rhineland.

von Neumann, J. and Morgenstern, O., *Theory of Games and Economic Behaviour* (3rd ed. 1953), Princeton University Press.

Zeleny, M., *Multiple Criteria Decision Making* (1982), McGraw-Hill.

Chapter 9 Network Analysis

Kharbanda, O. P. and Stallworthy, E. A., *How to Learn From Project Disasters* (1983), Gower Press.

Lee, S. M., Moeller, G. L. and Digman, L. A., *Network Analysis for Management Decisions: A Stochastic Approach* (1982), Kluwer-Nijhoff Publishing.

Lester, A., *Project Planning and Control* (1982), Butterworth Scientific Publishers.

Lockyer, K., *Critical Path Analysis and Other Project Network Techniques* (1984), Pitman Publishing.

Smith, D. K., *Network Optimisation Practice: A Computational Guide* (1982), Ellis Horwood.

Chapter 10 Dynamic Programming

Kallenberg, L. C. M., *Linear Programming and Finite Markovian Control Problems* (1983), Mathematisch Centrum.

White, D. J., *Optimality and Efficiency* (1982), John Wiley and Sons.

Whittle, P., *Optimization Over Time (Dynamic Programming and Stochastic Control, Volume 1)* (1982), John Wiley and Sons.

Index

Index